Royal Flash ™

Cort's Royal Ink Tattoo Company
Presents
"Religous Tattoos"
All Artwork by
Cort Bengtson

Published by

Cort's Royal Ink Tattoo Company

Book Design and Layout by

Cort Bengtson

Copyright 2017

All images are on file with

The Library of Congress

All rights reserved. No part of this publication may be reproduced, stored in a digital format or reproduced in any form or by any means, electronic, mechanical, photographic or any other method of reproduction without advanced written permission from the publisher. ISBN-13: 978-1-948187-14-5

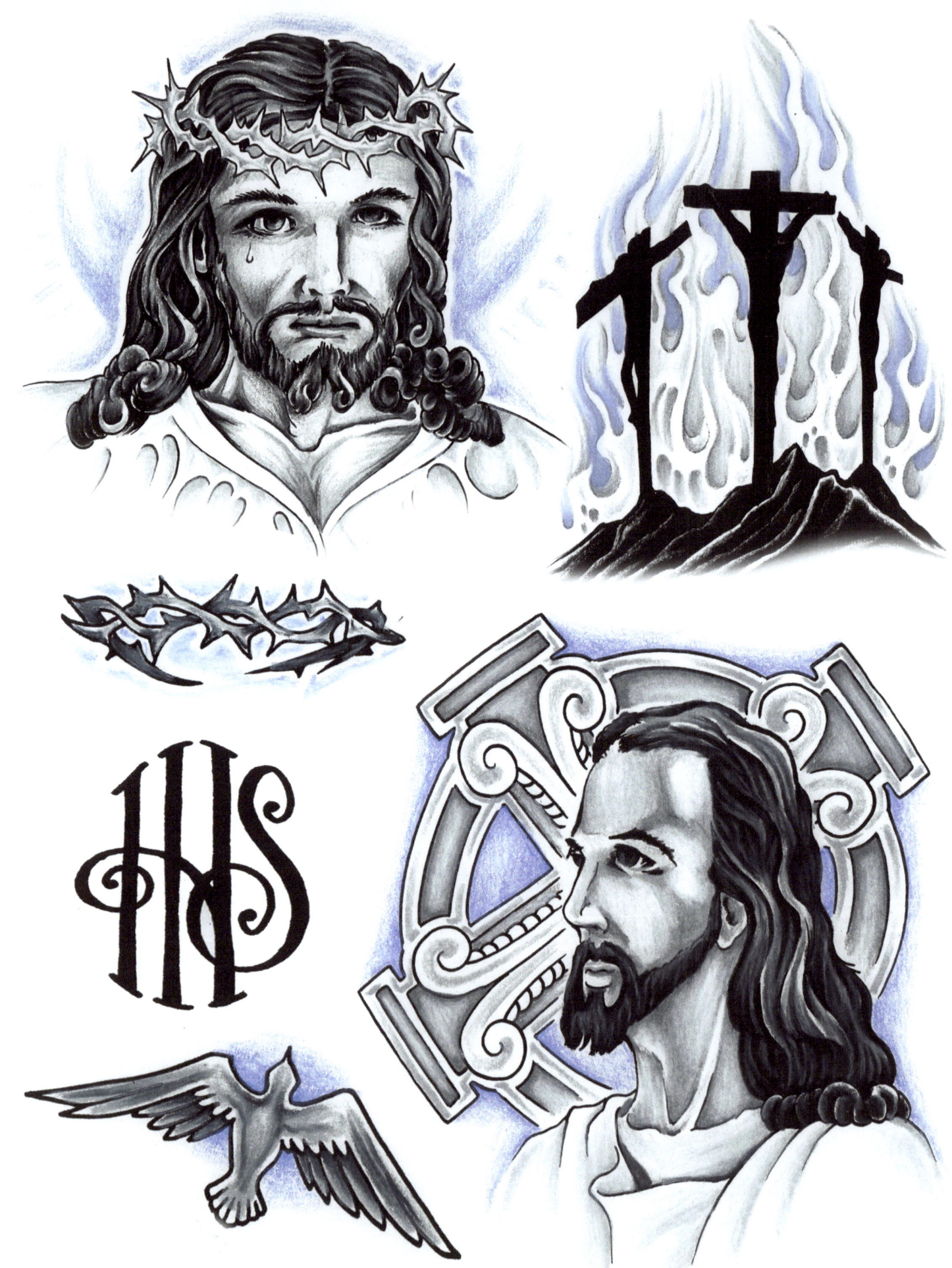

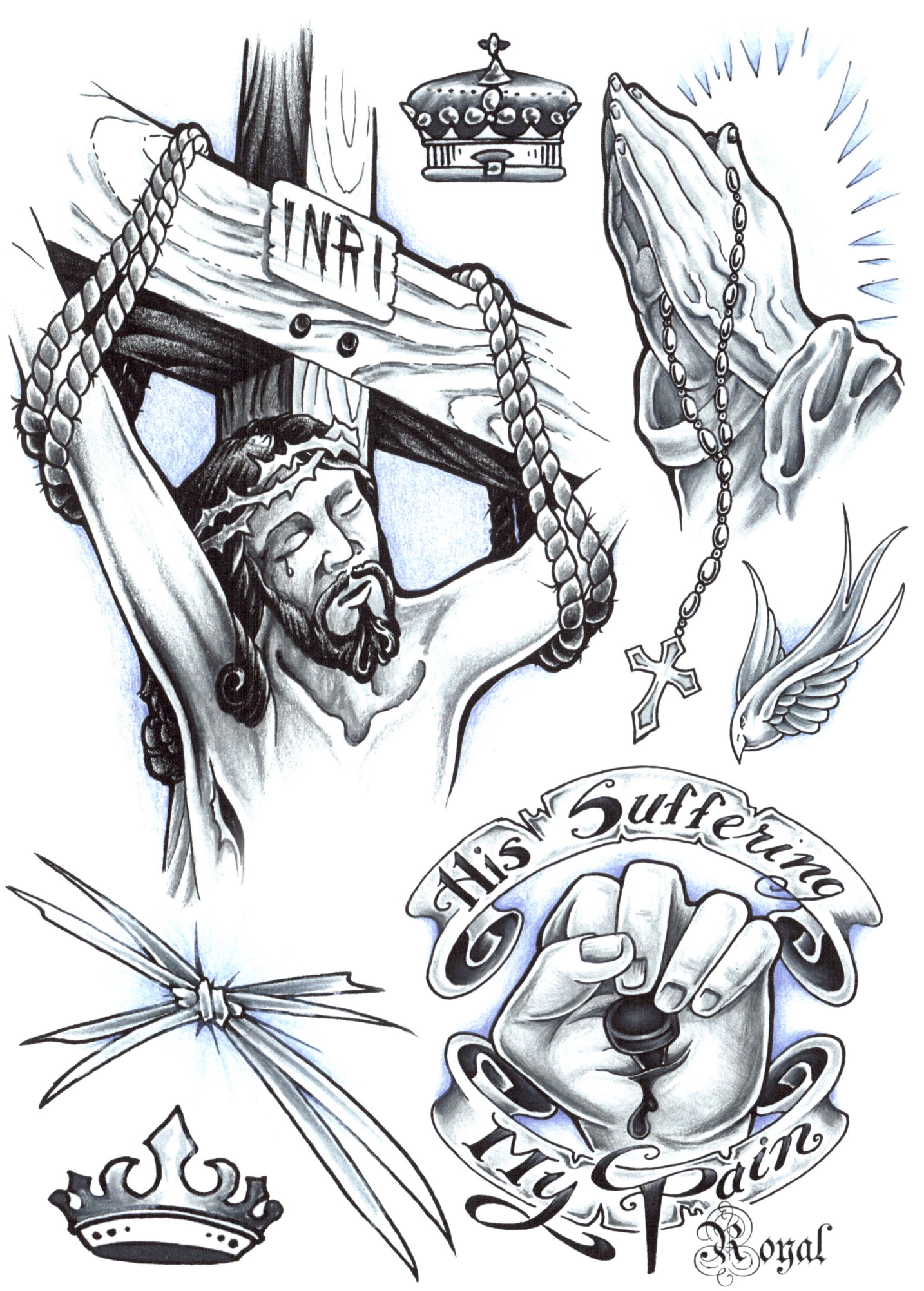

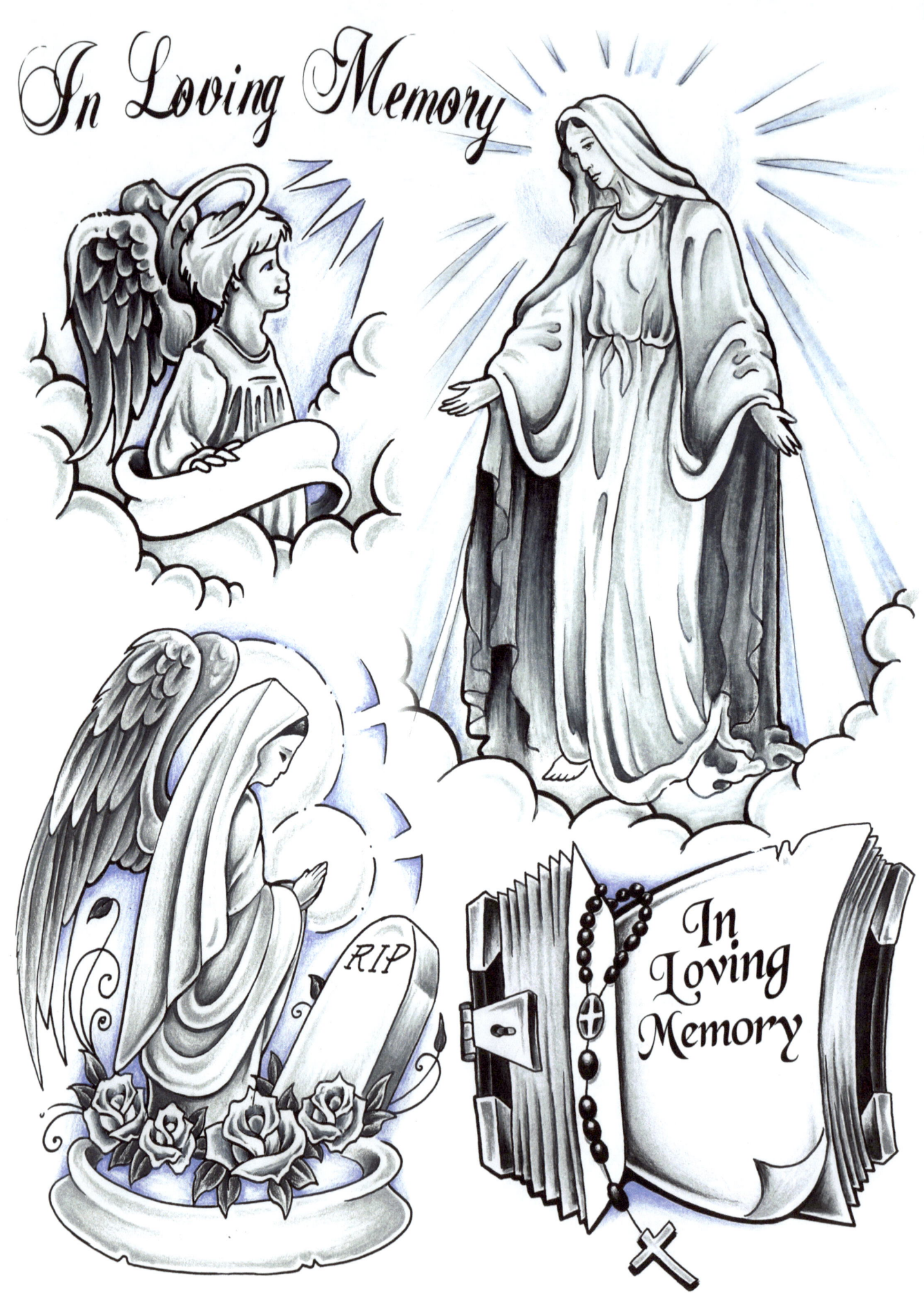

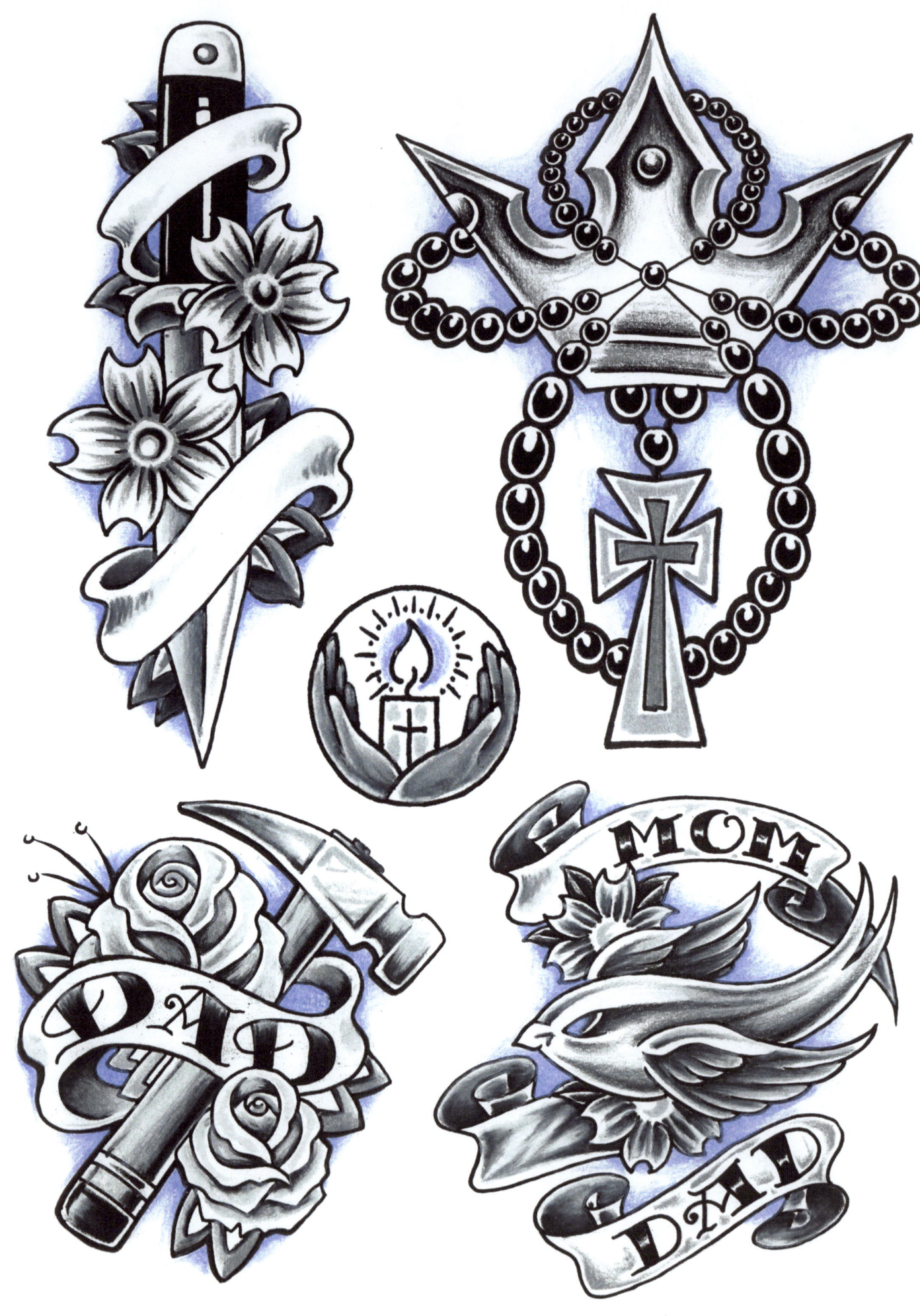

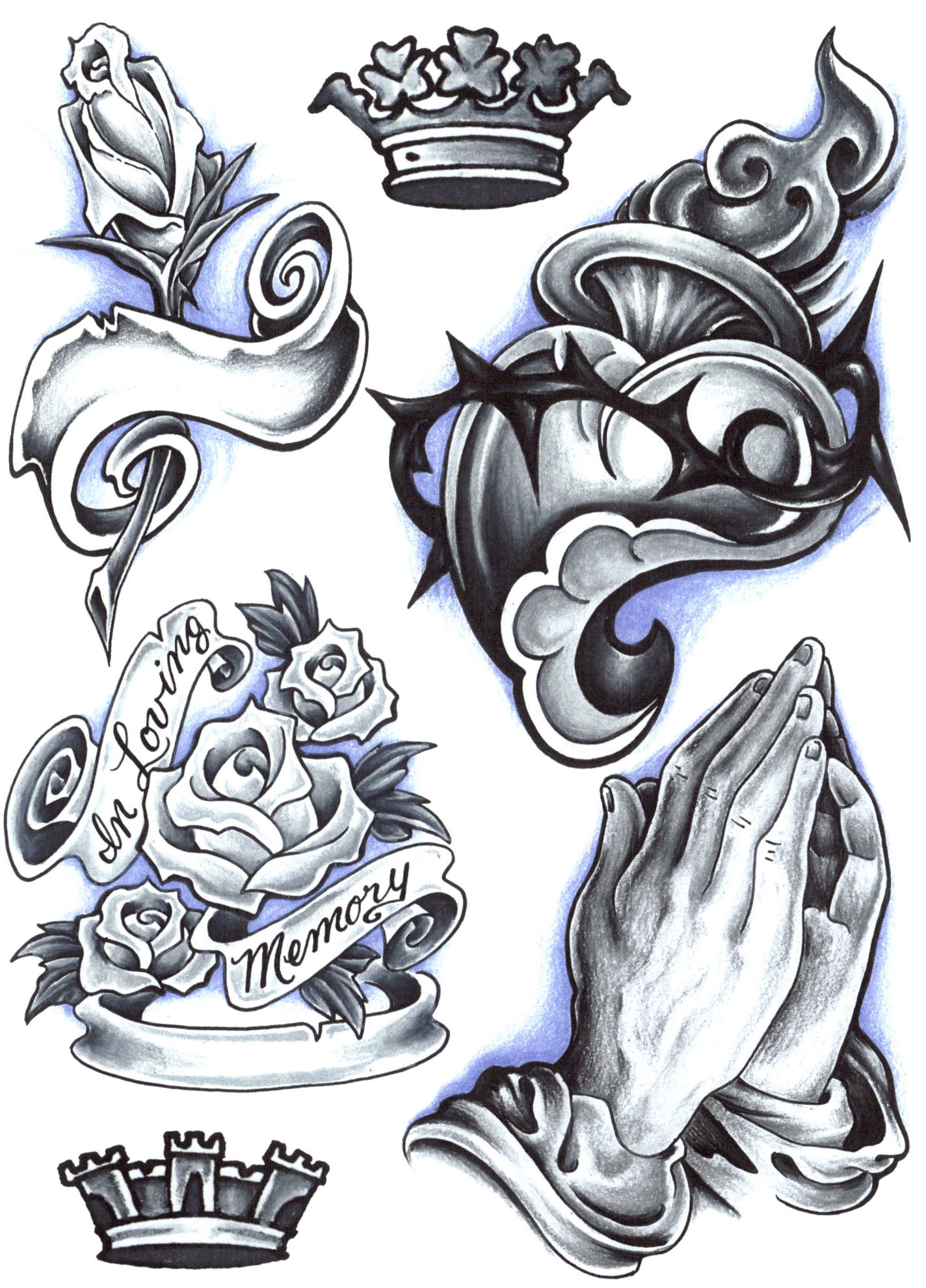

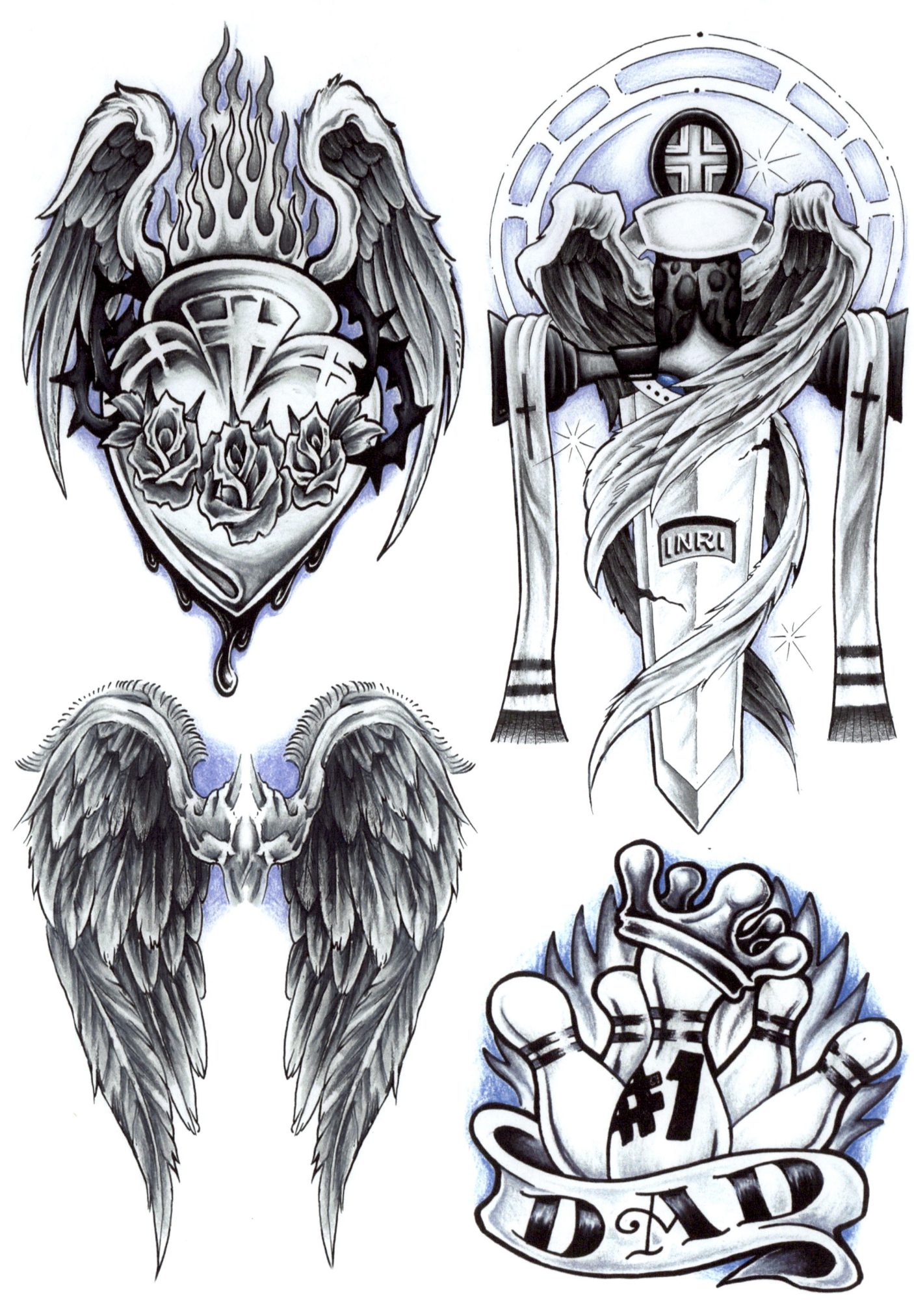

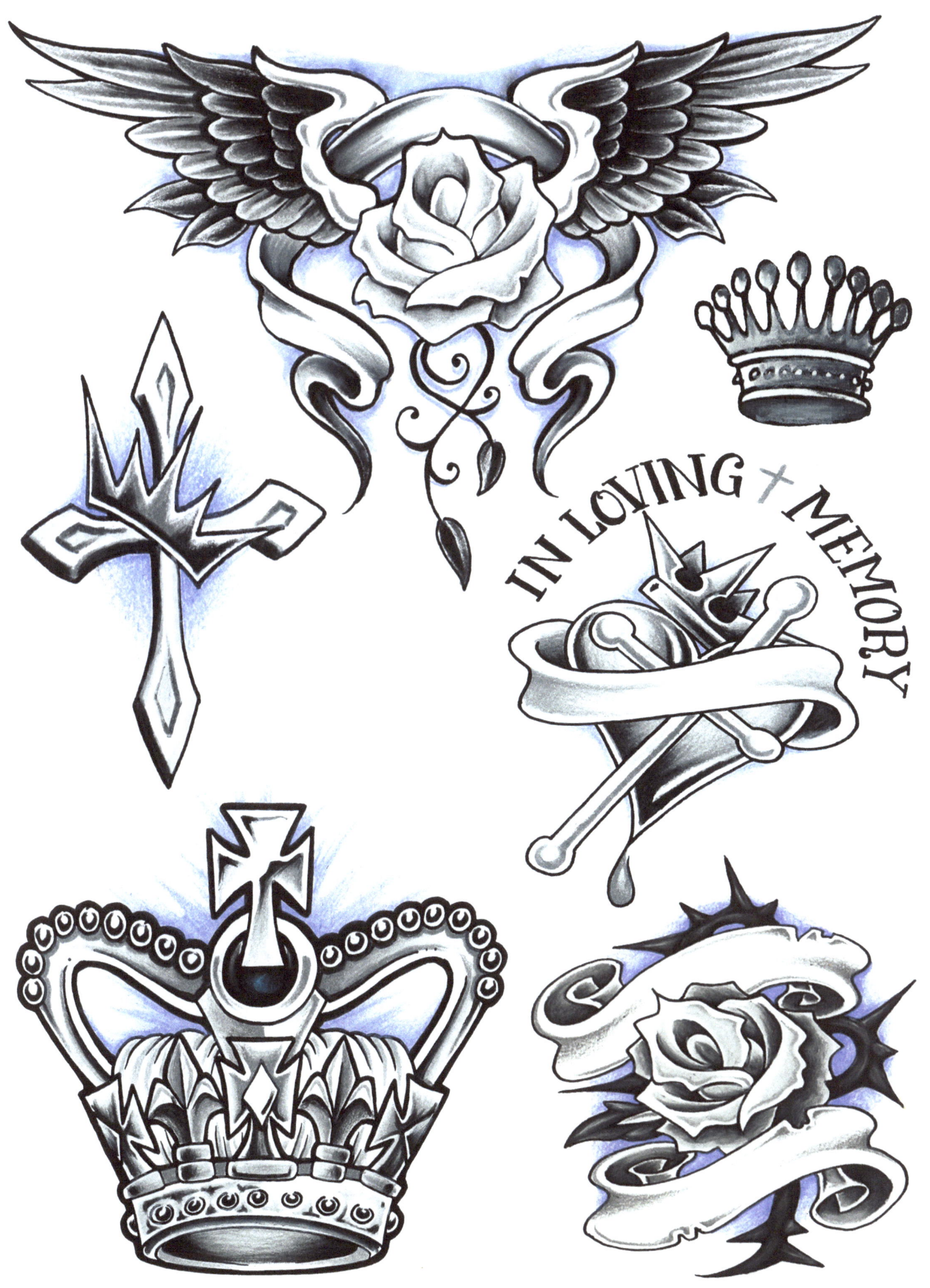

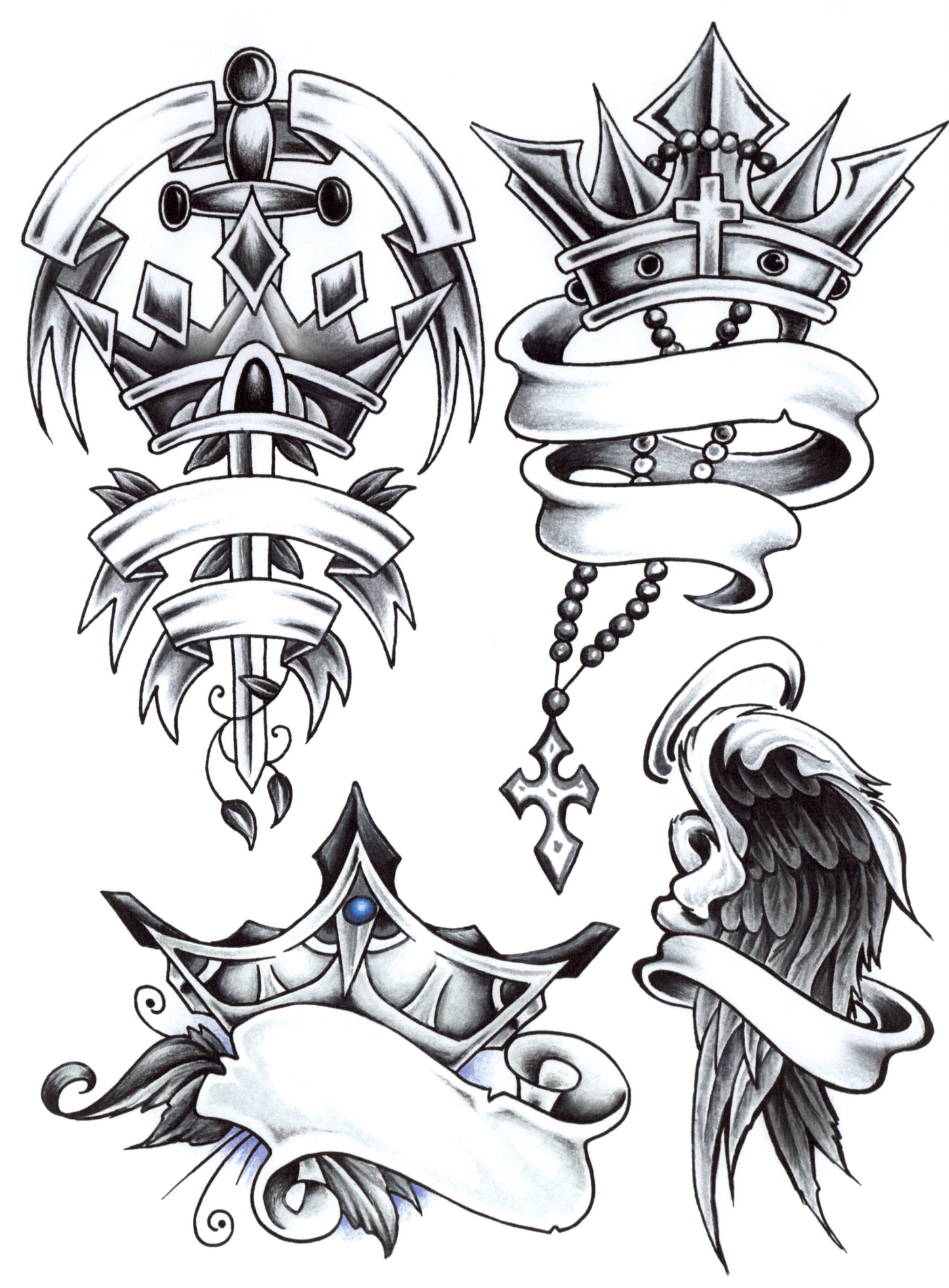

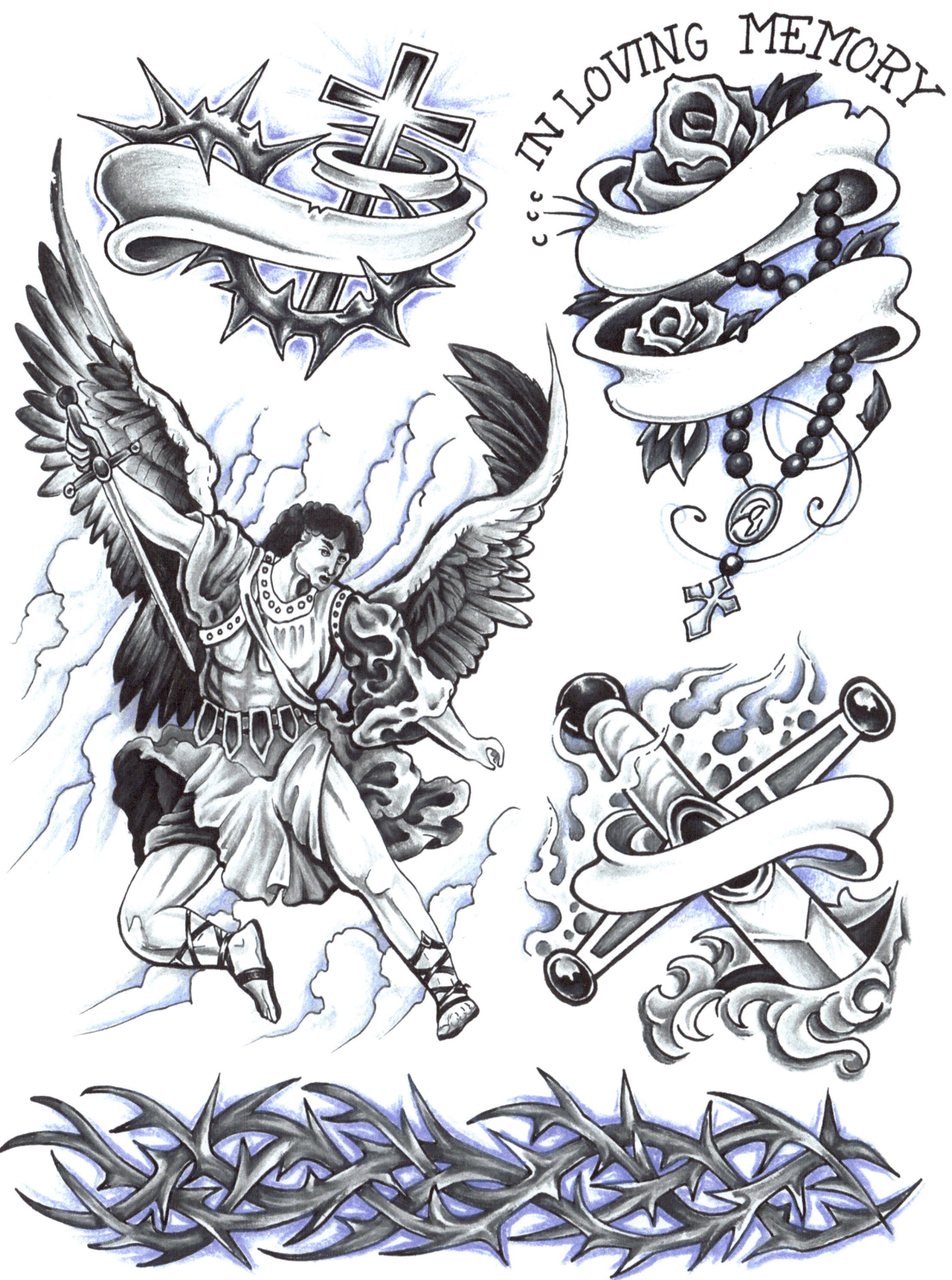

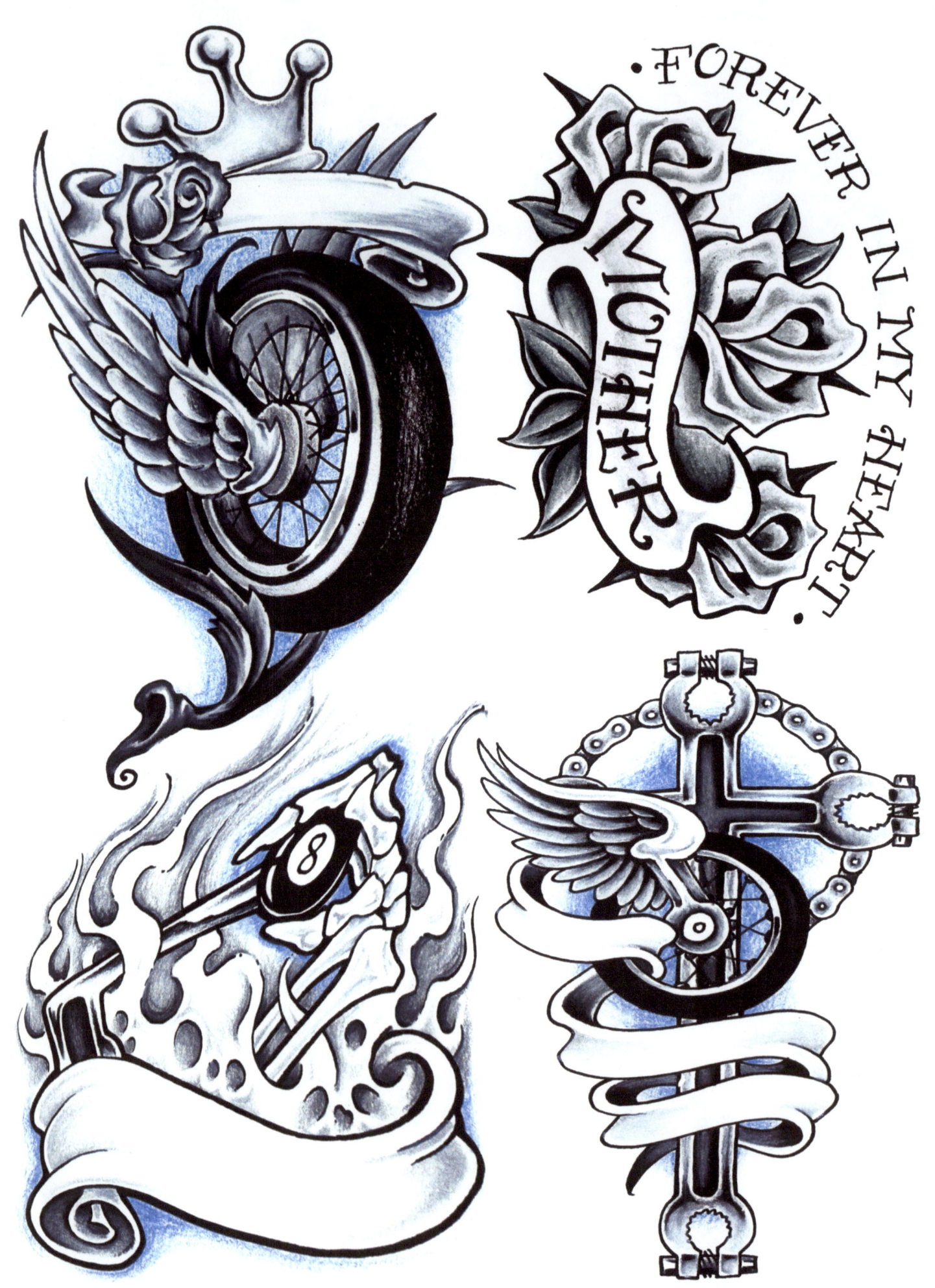

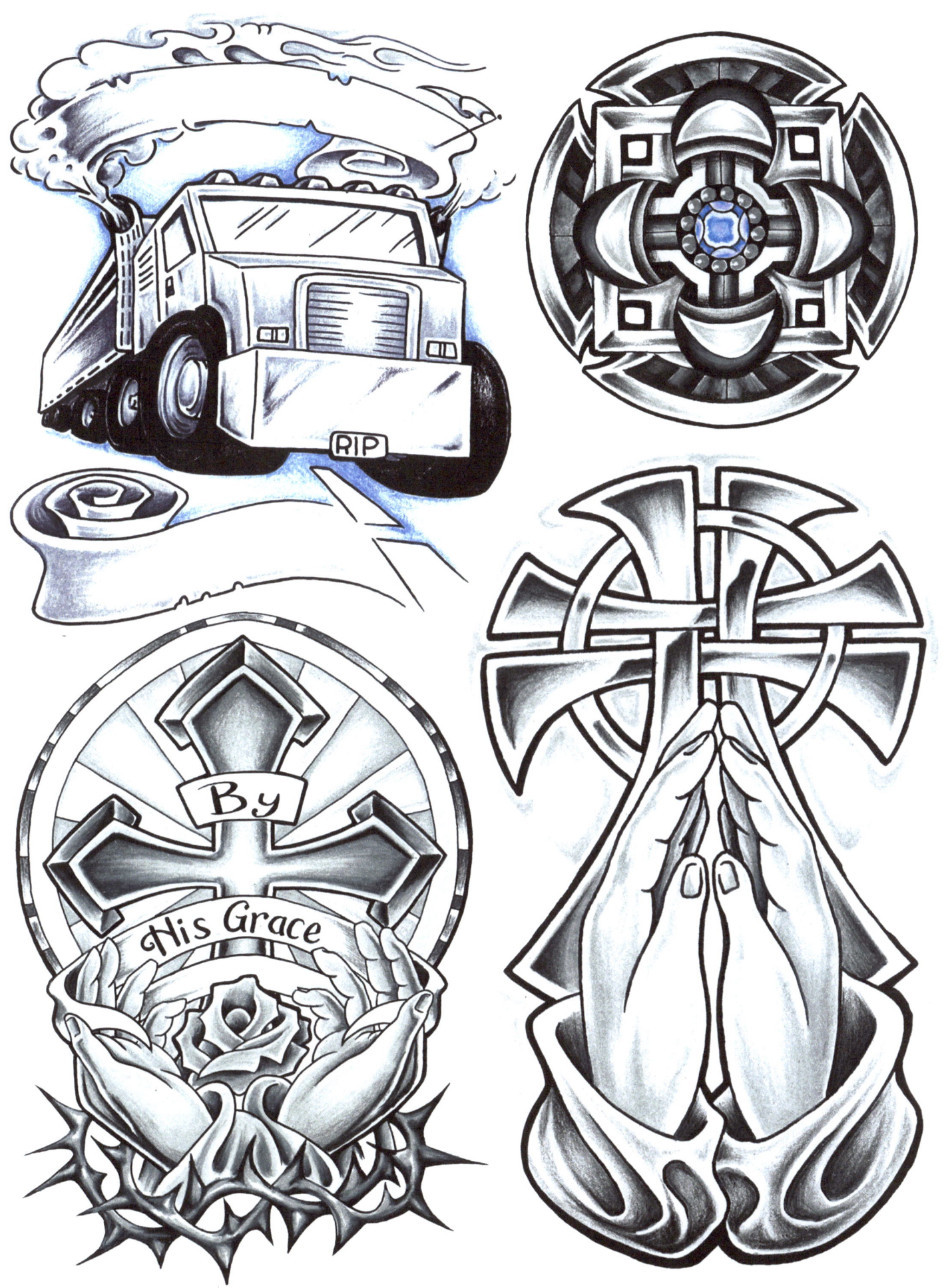

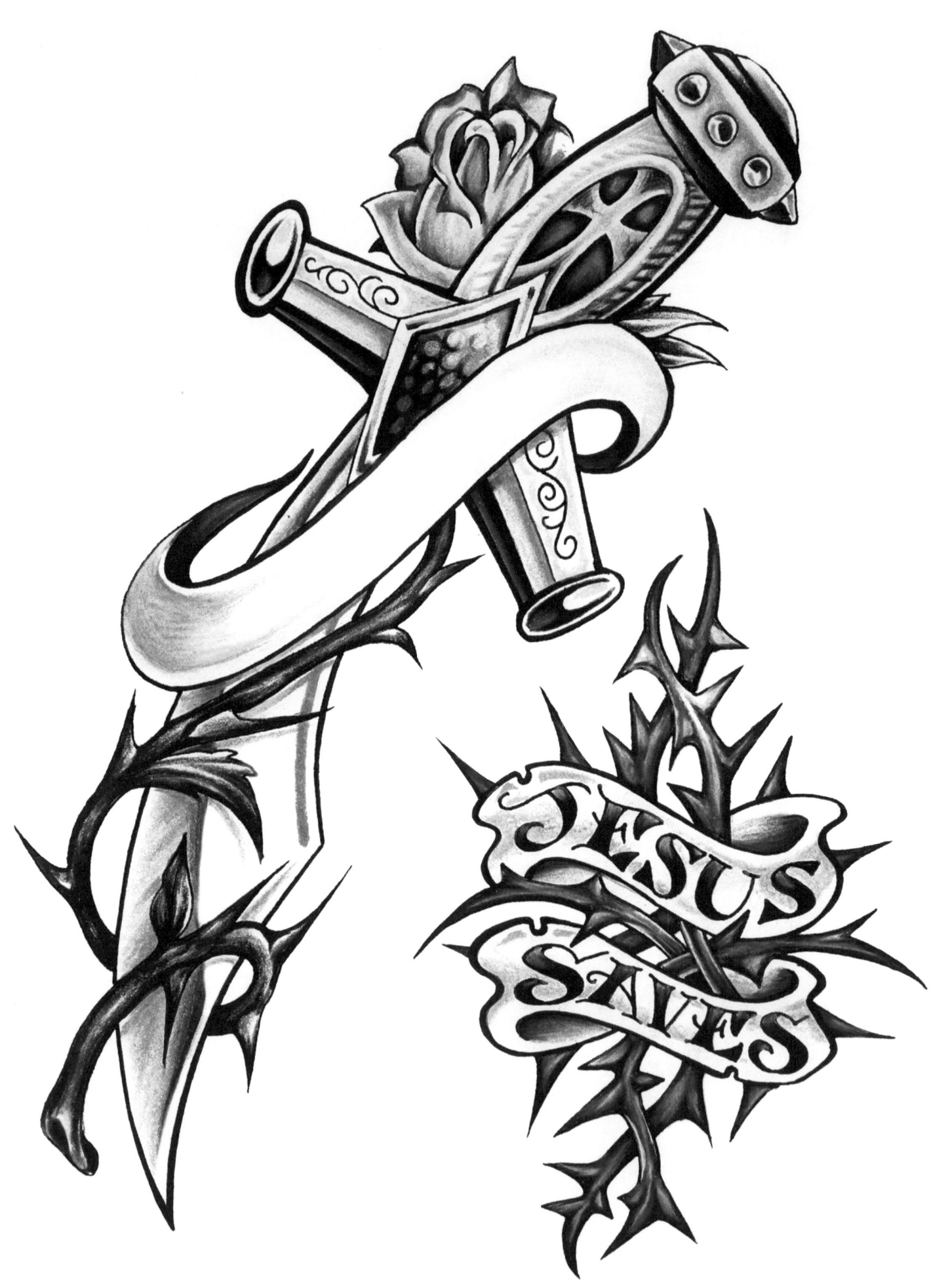

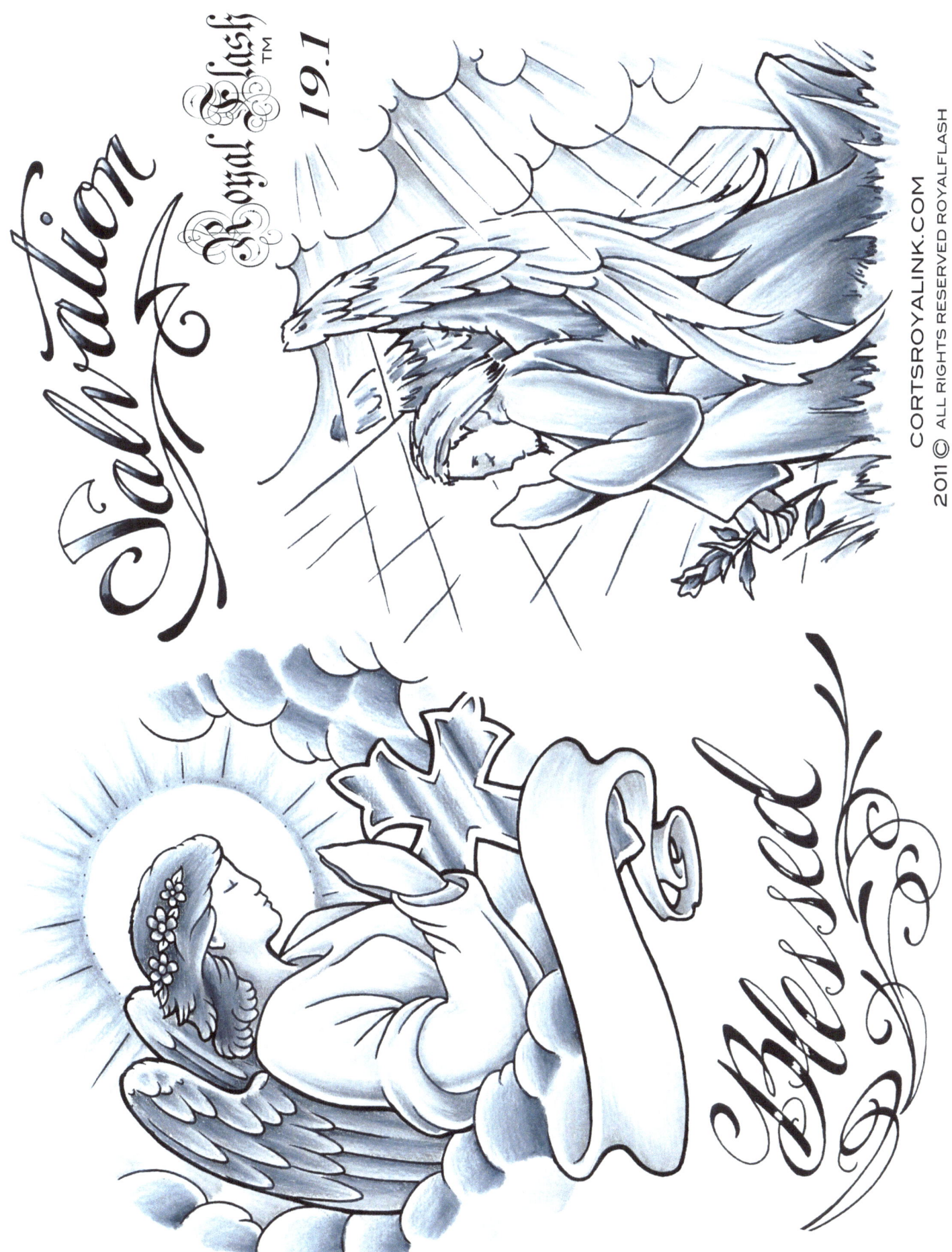

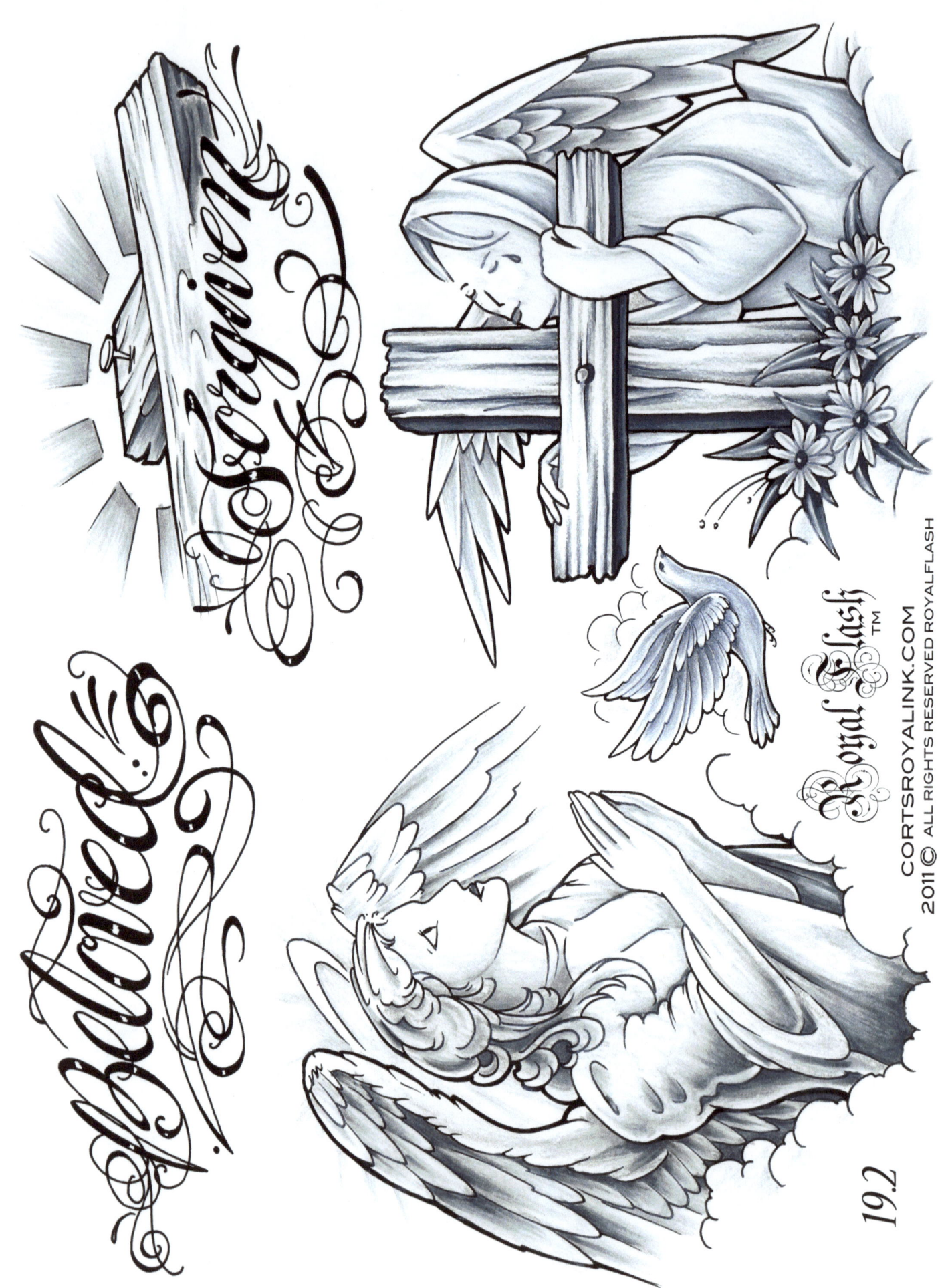

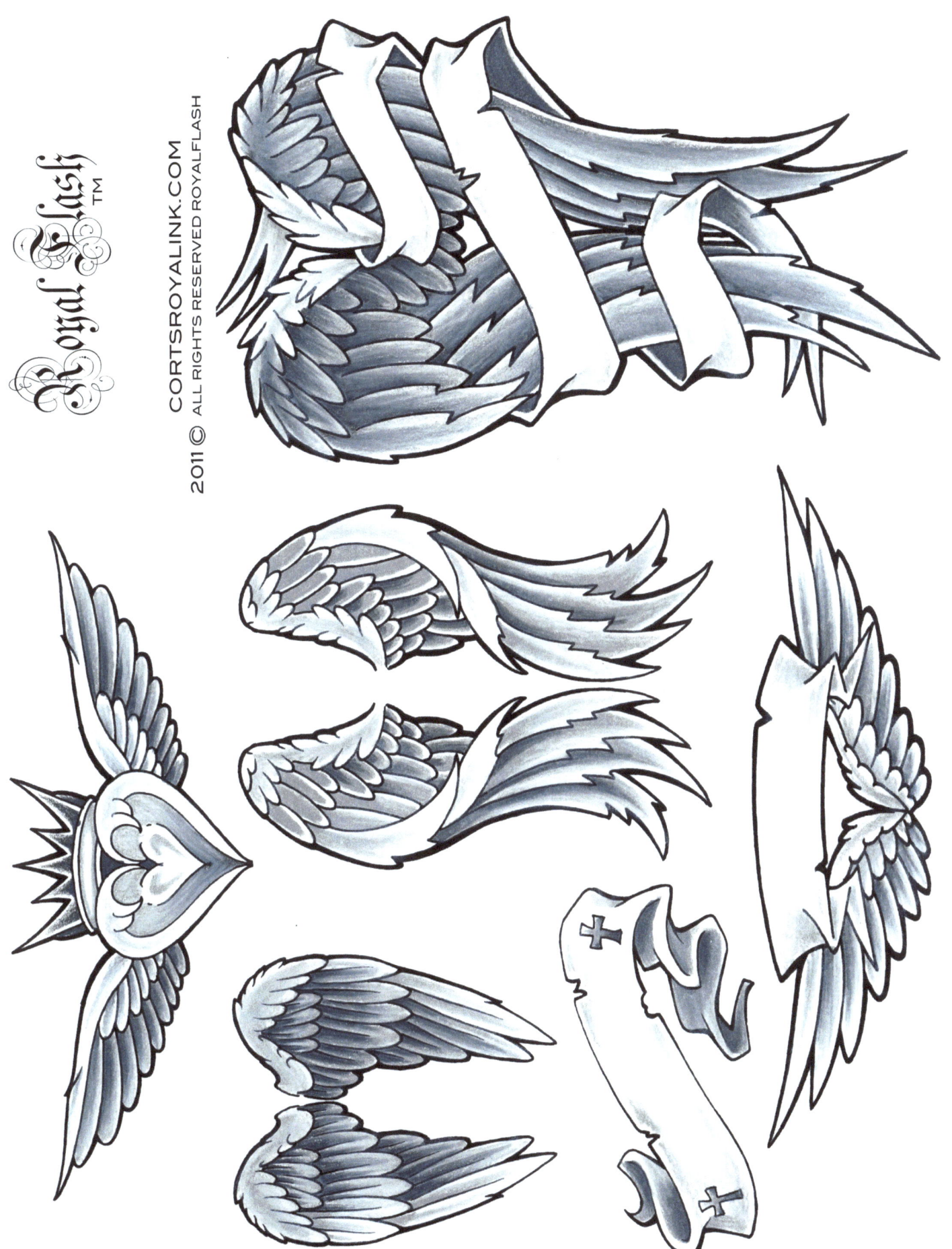

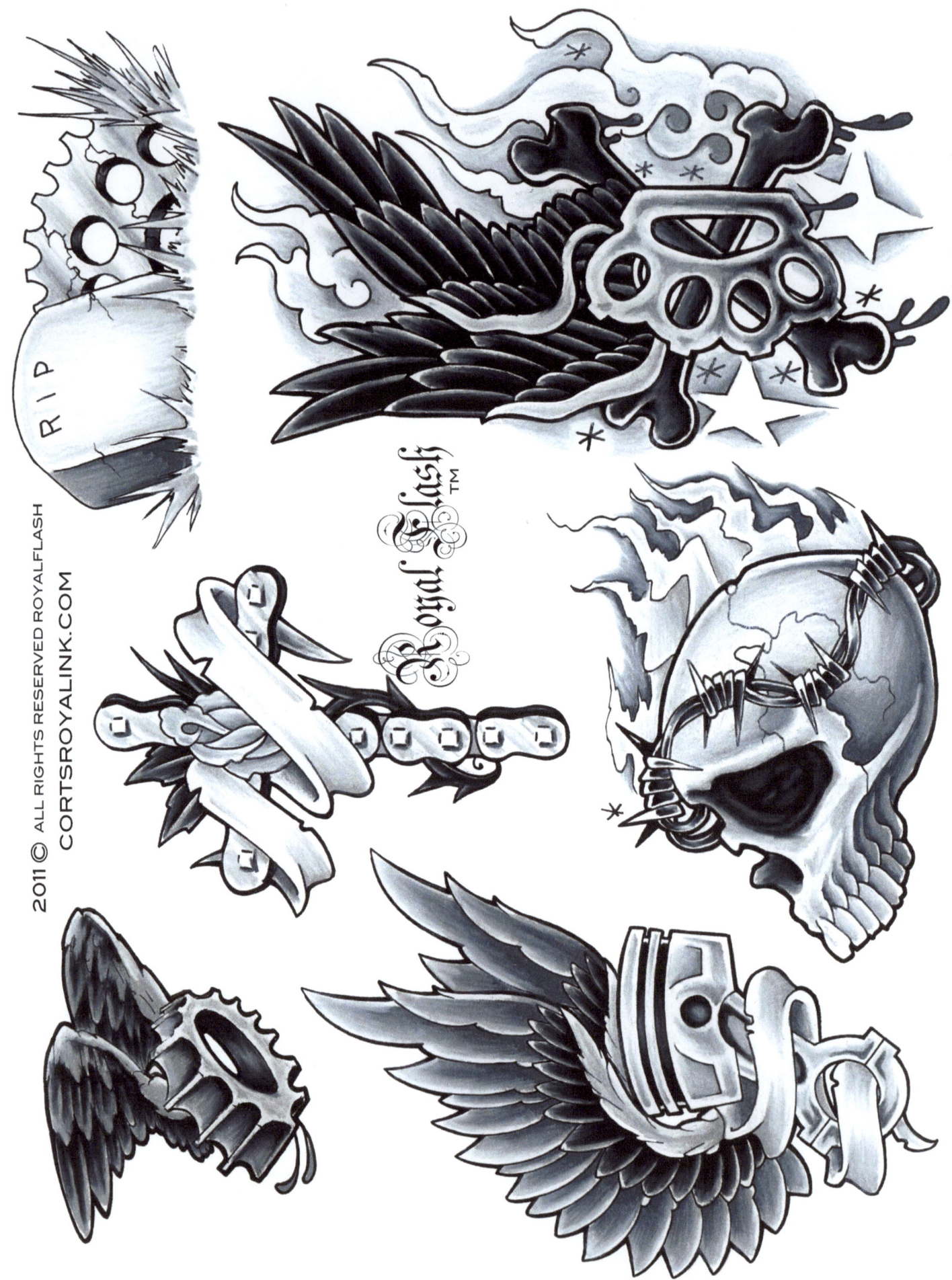

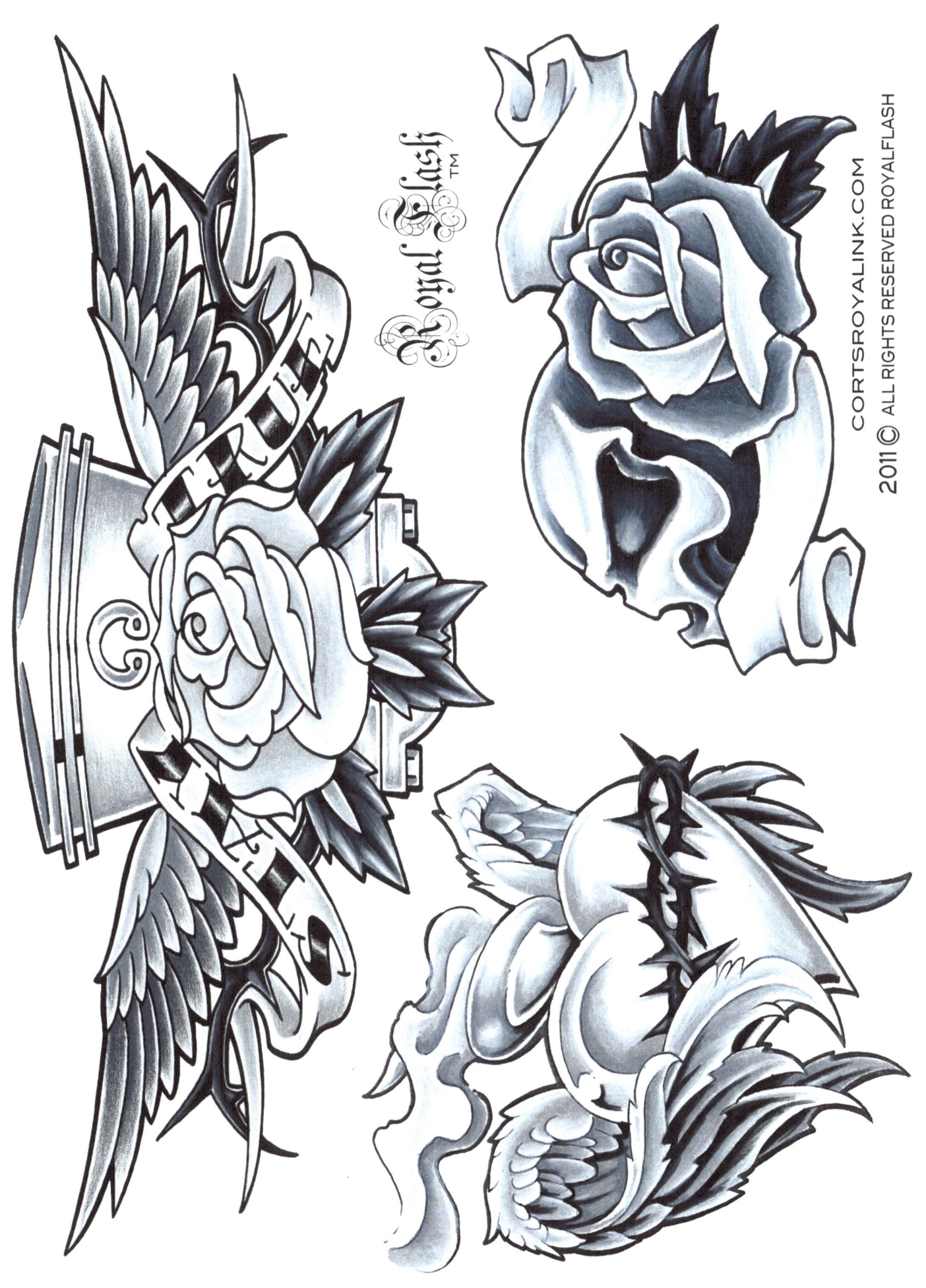

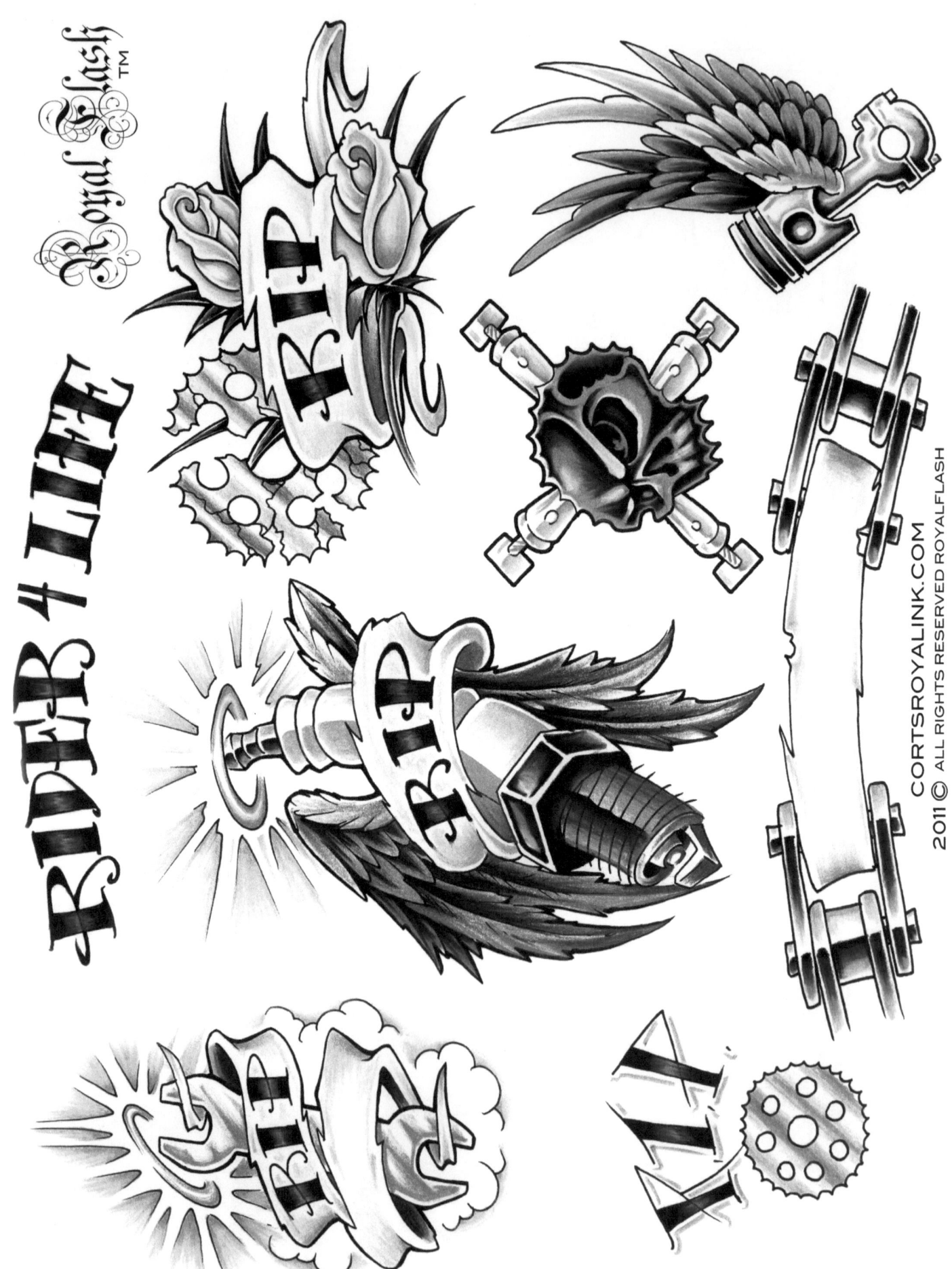

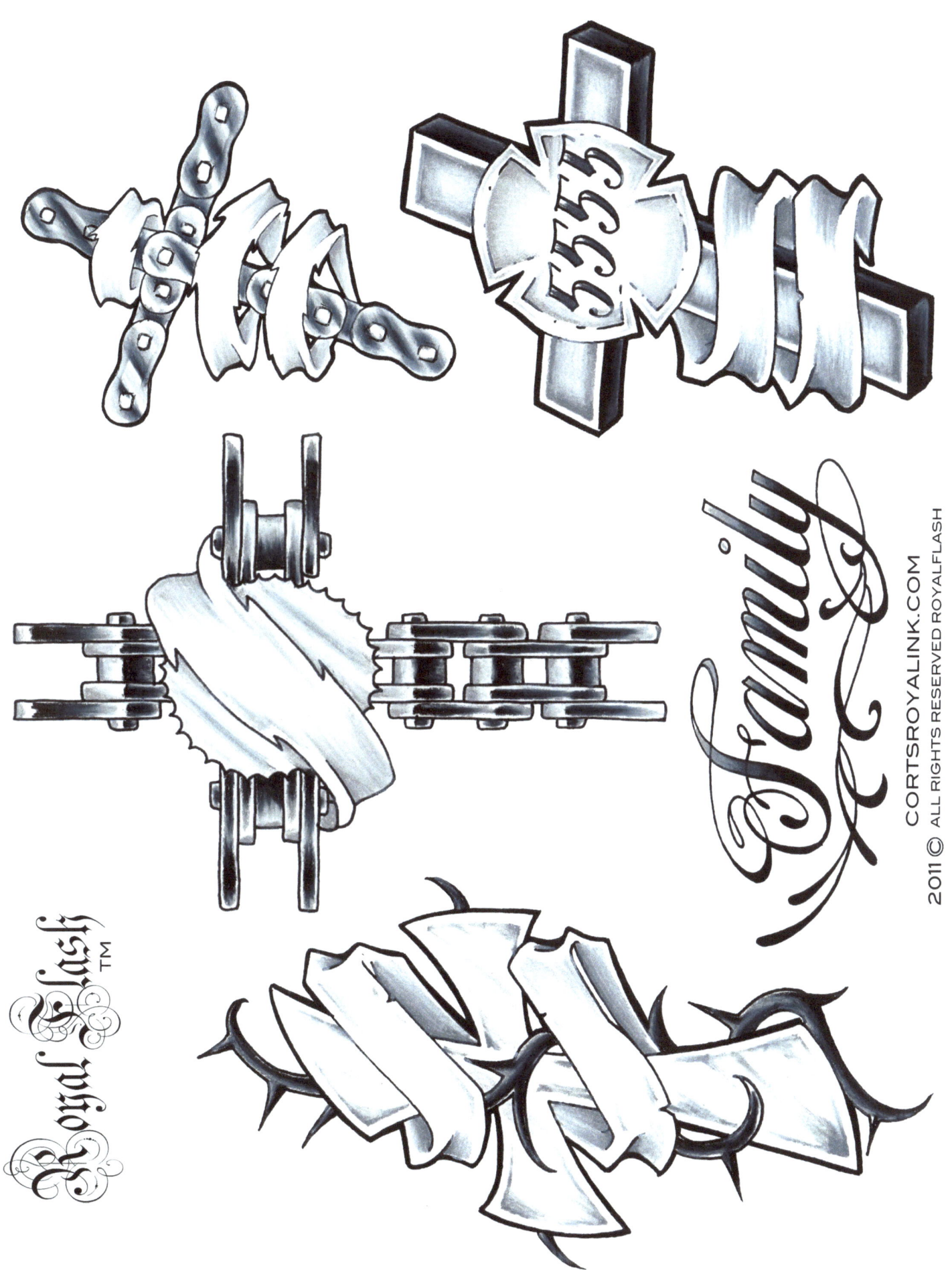

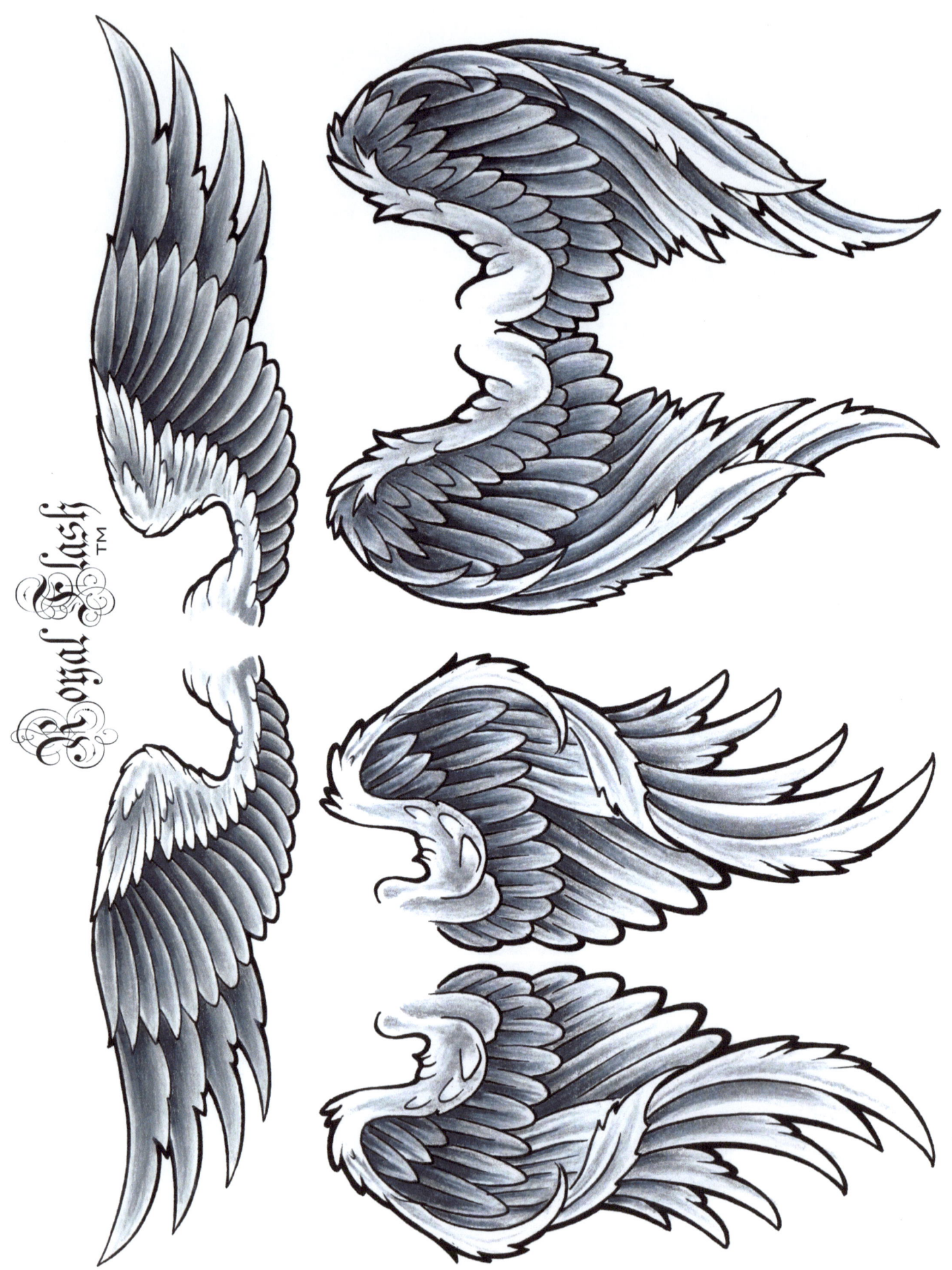

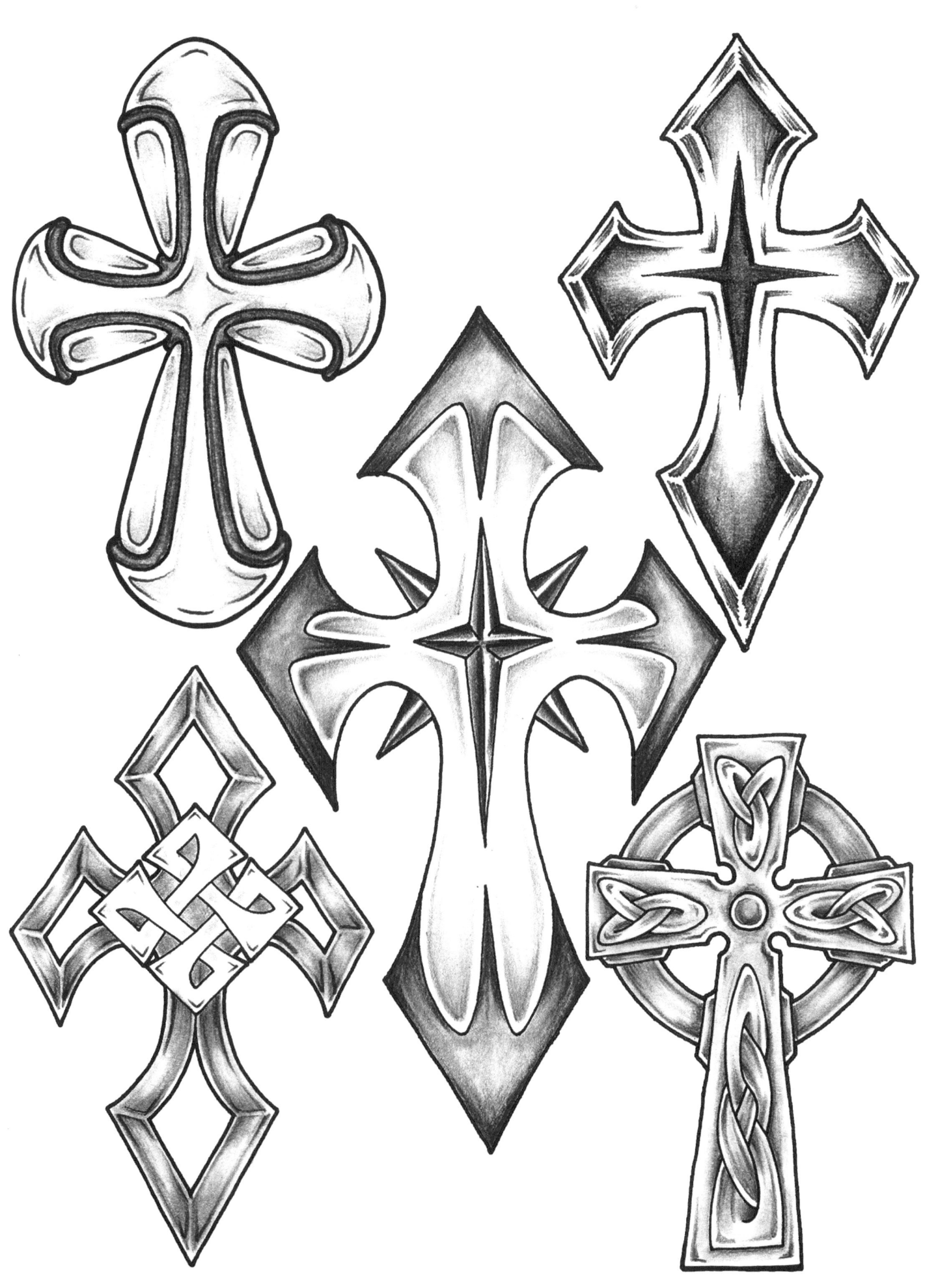

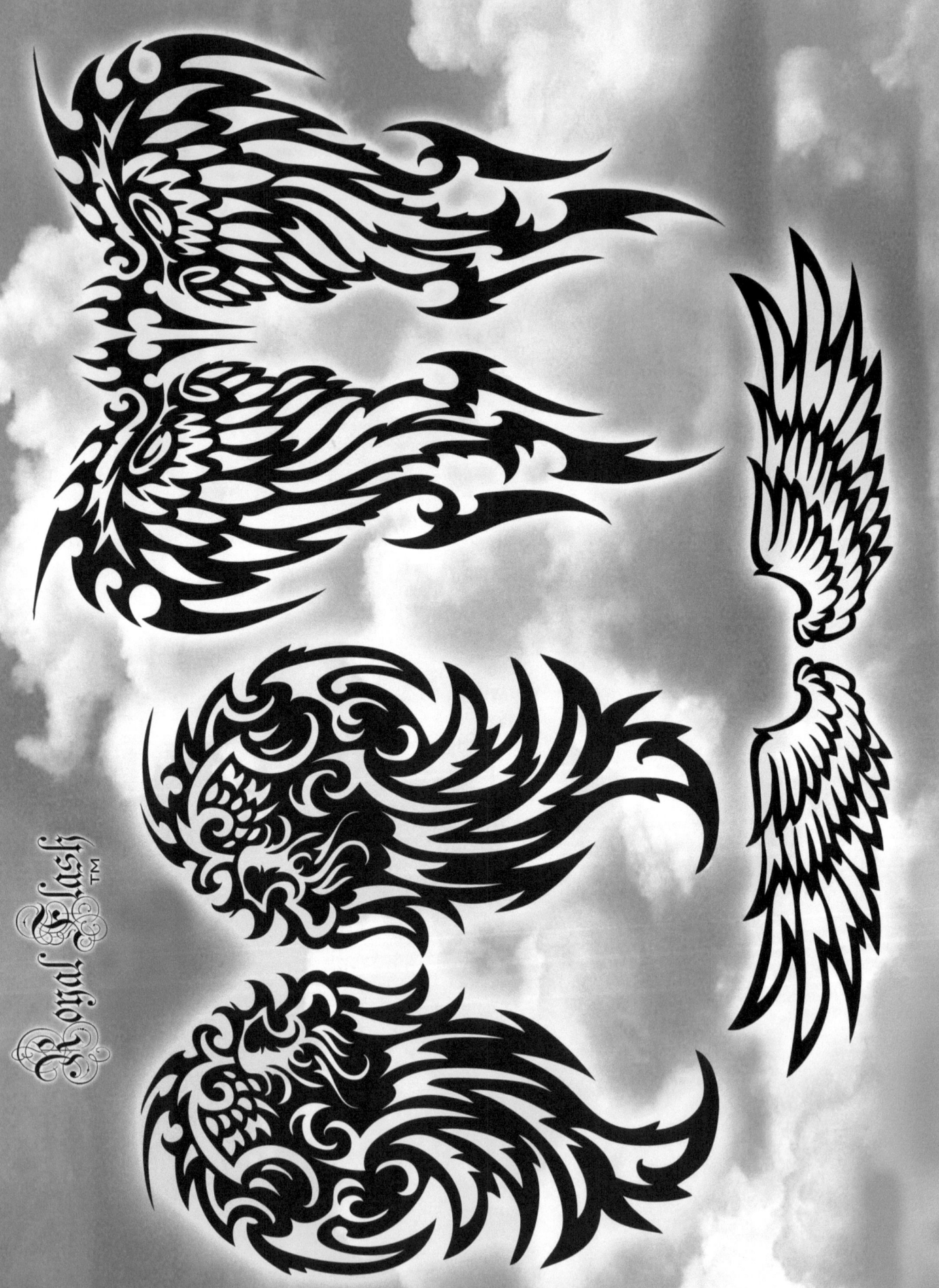

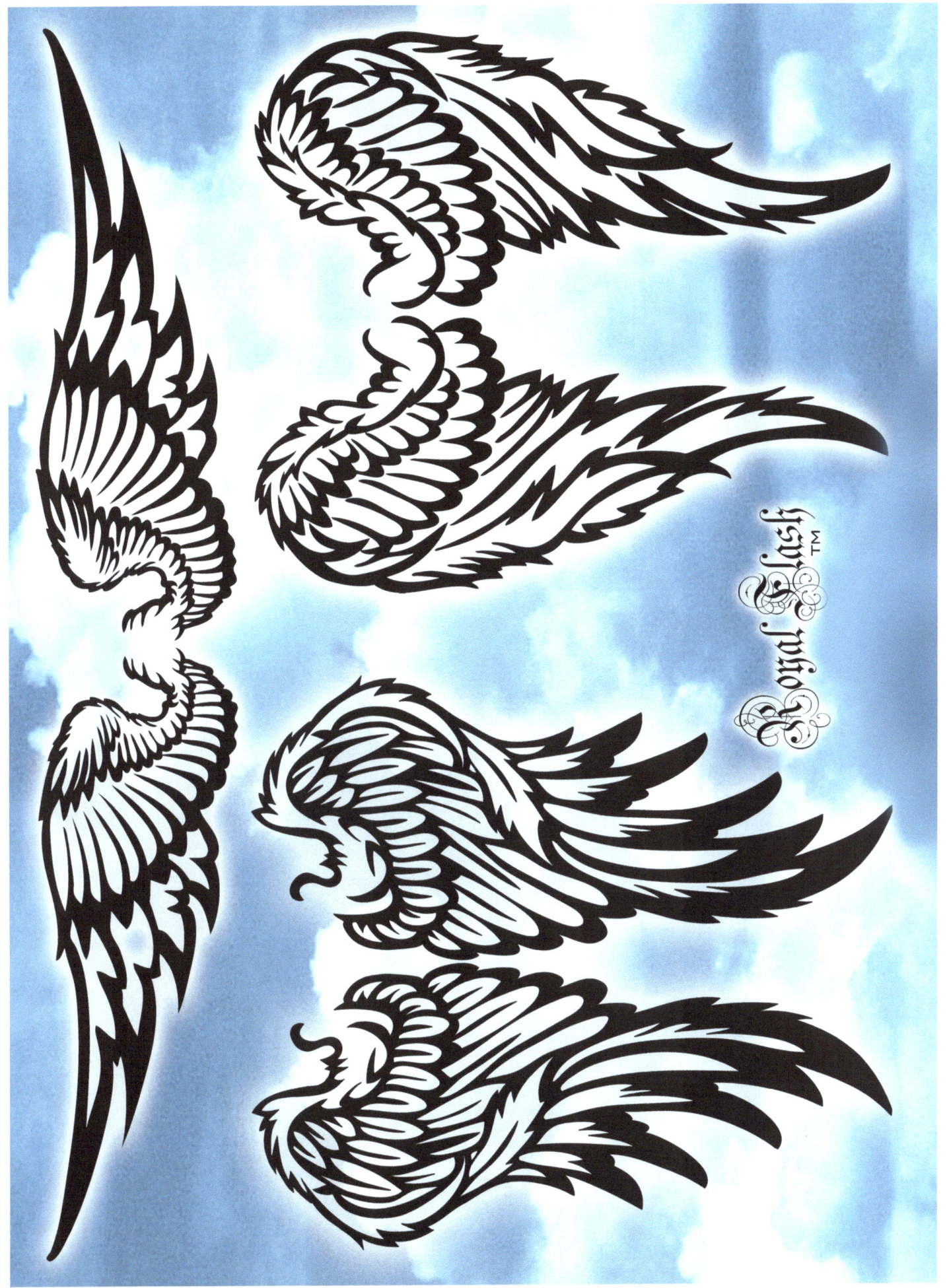

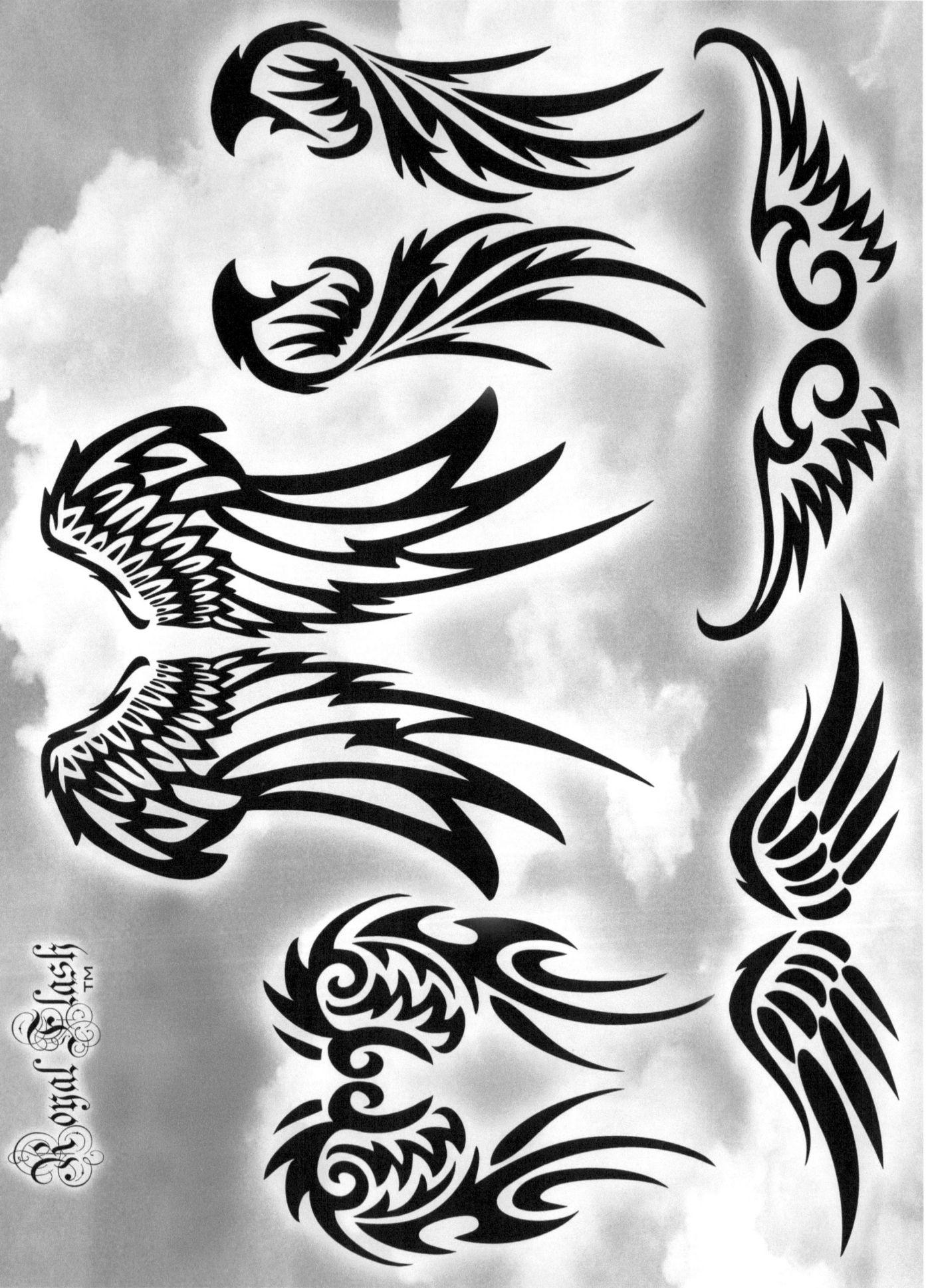

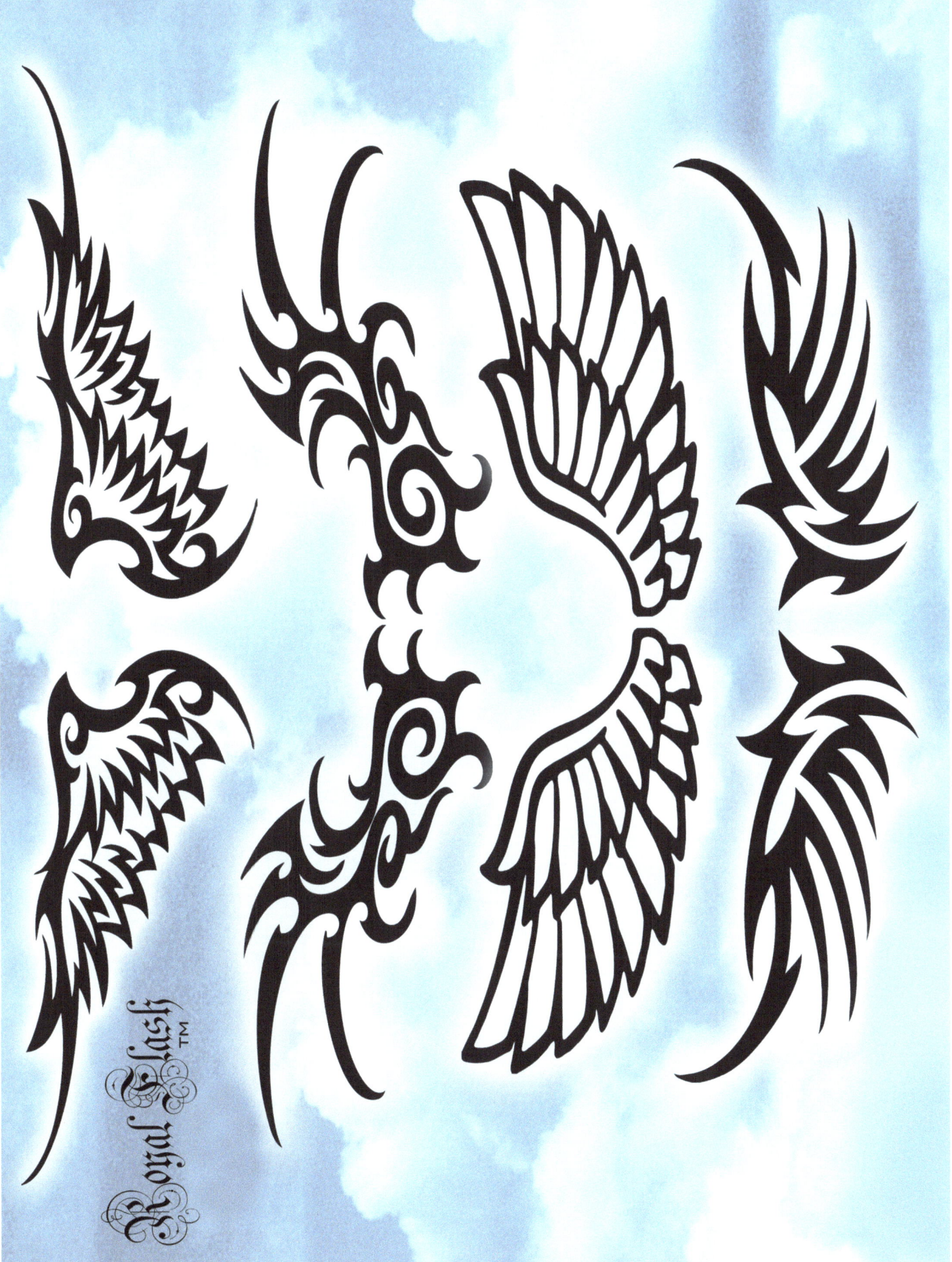

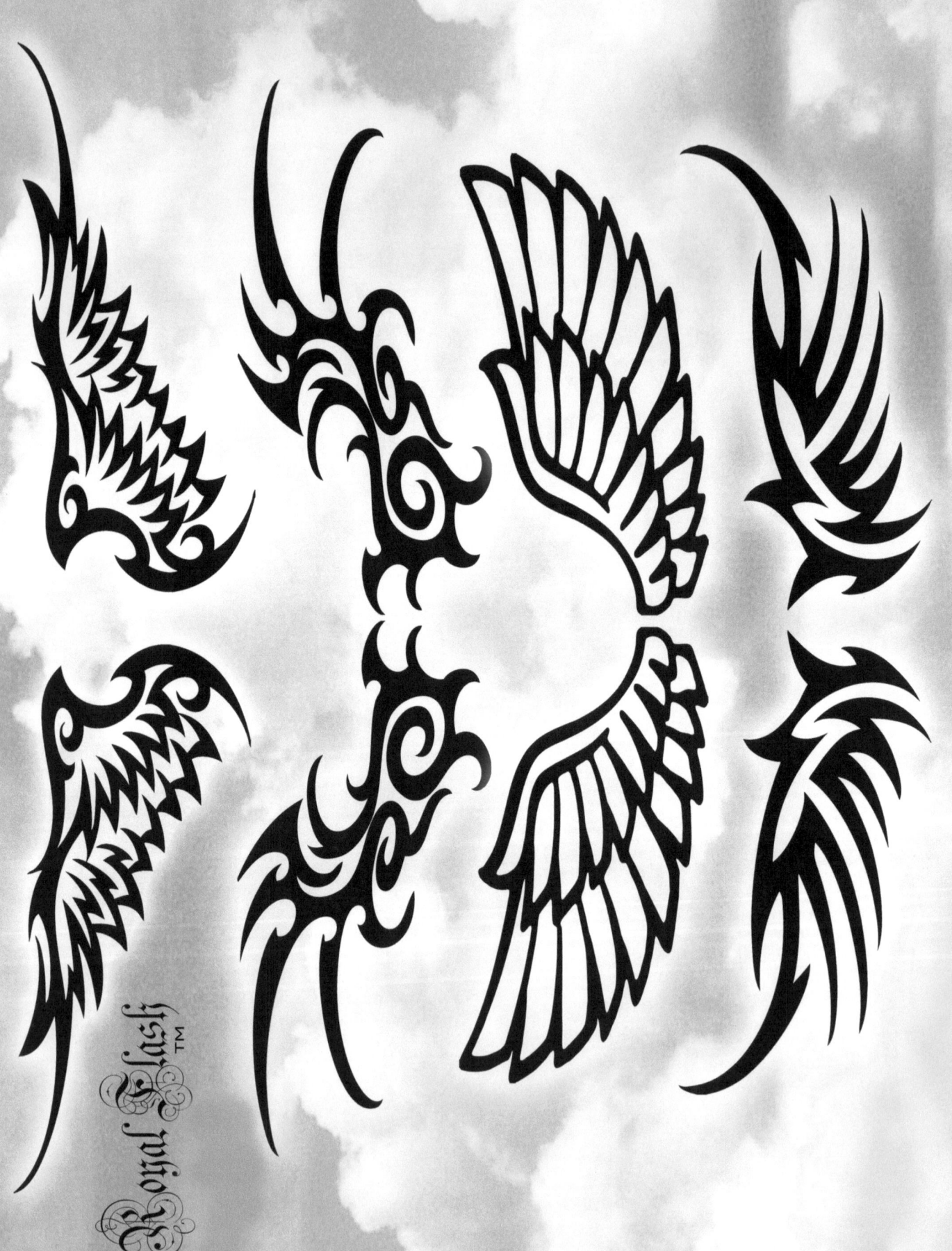

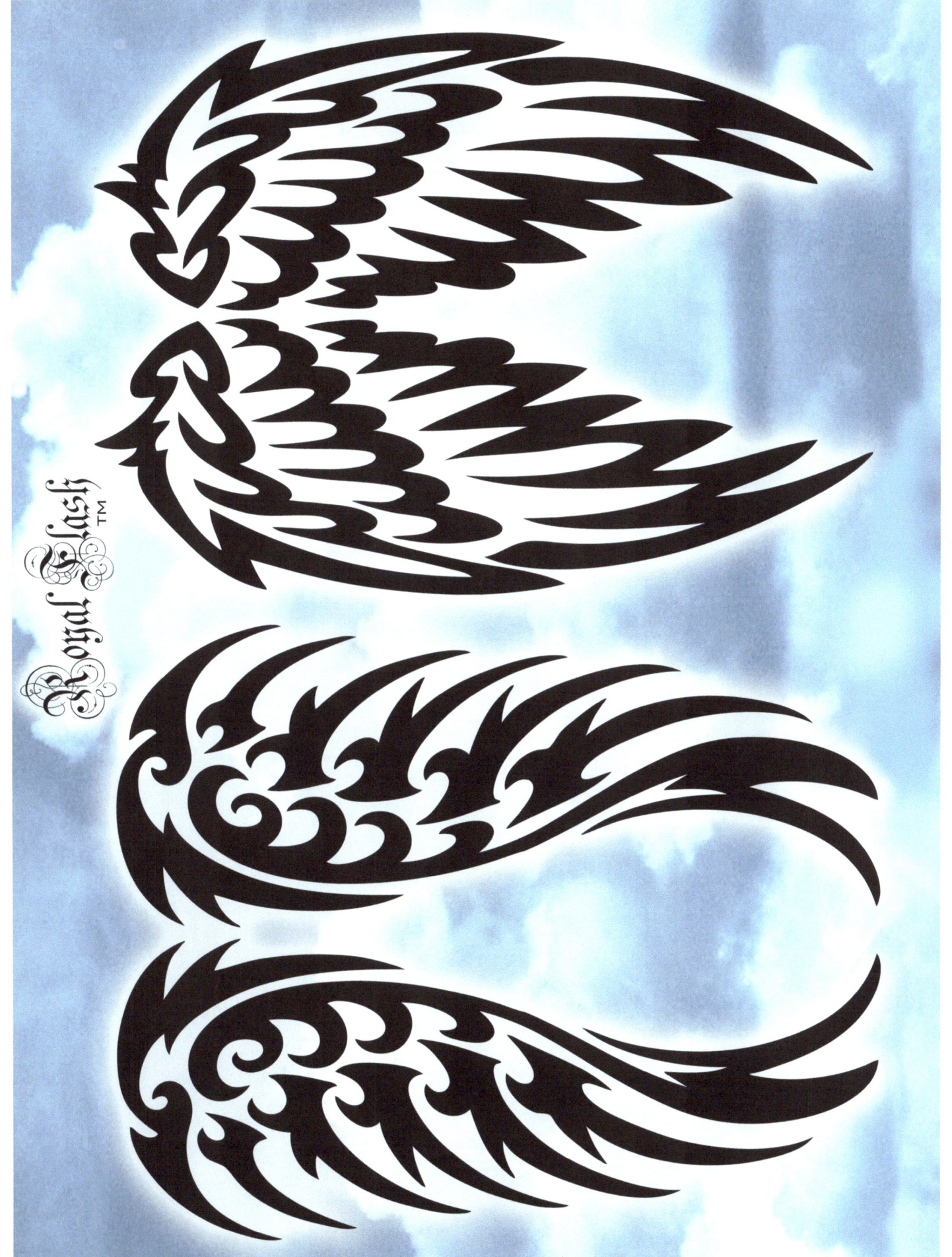

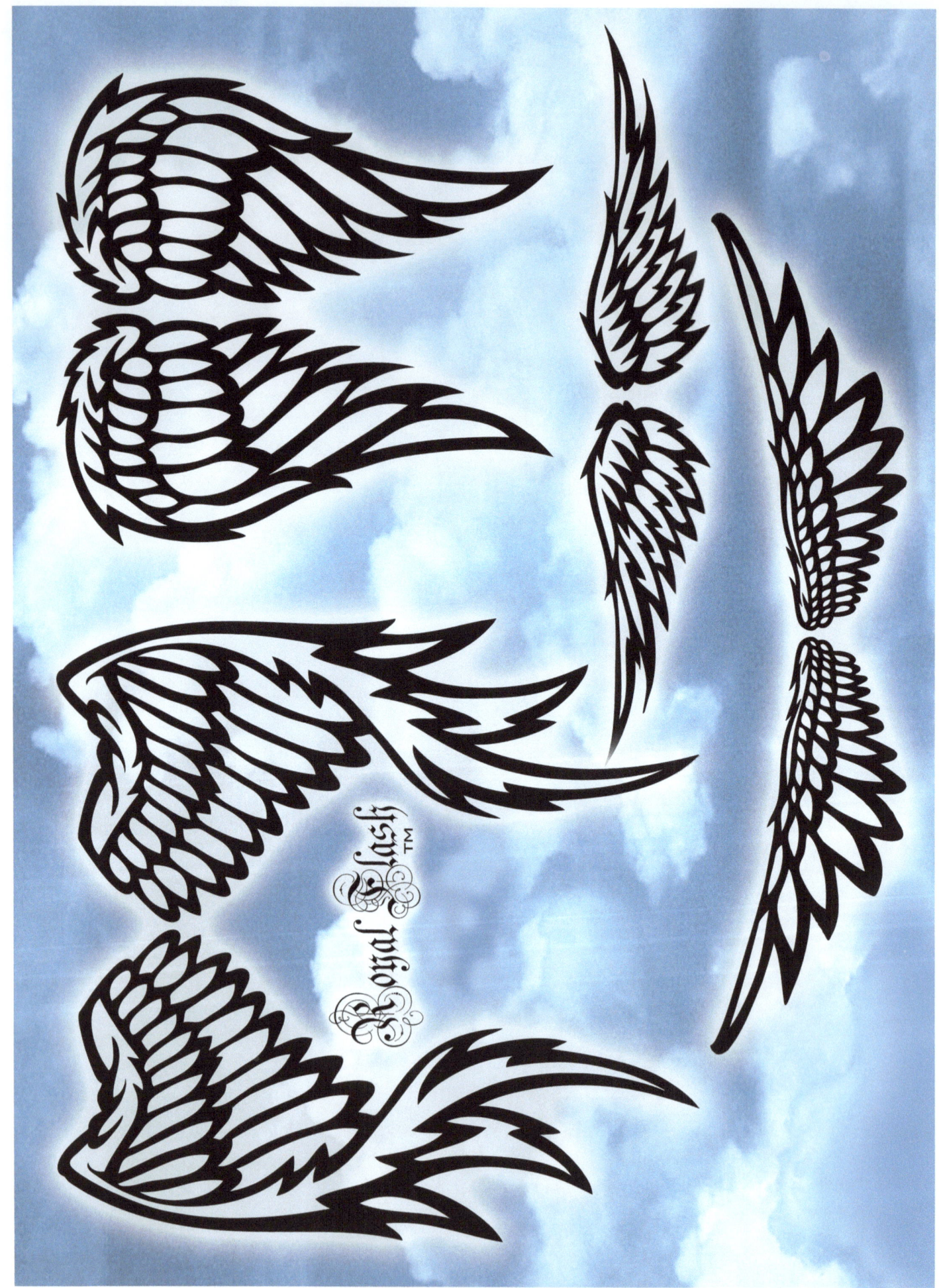

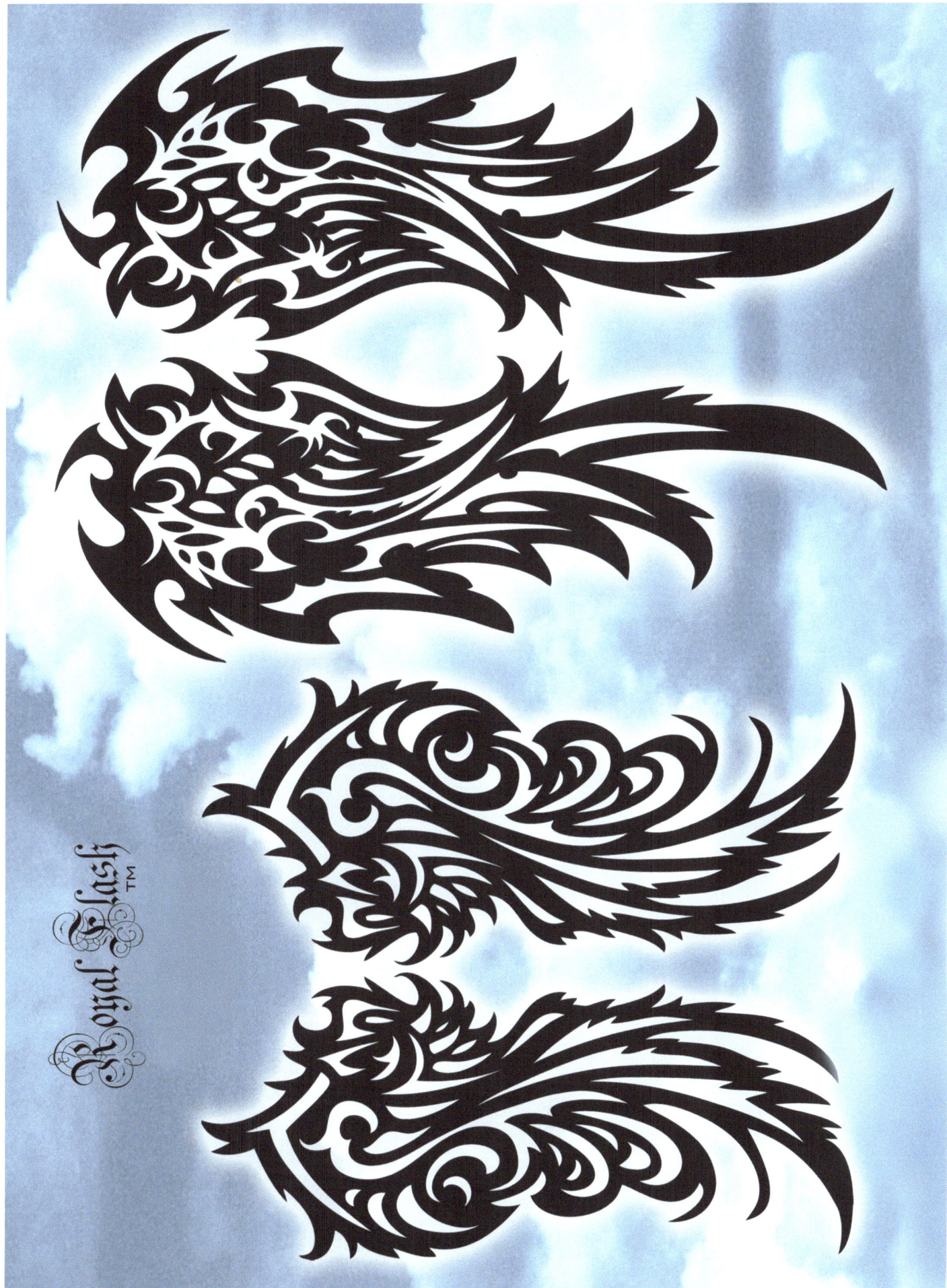

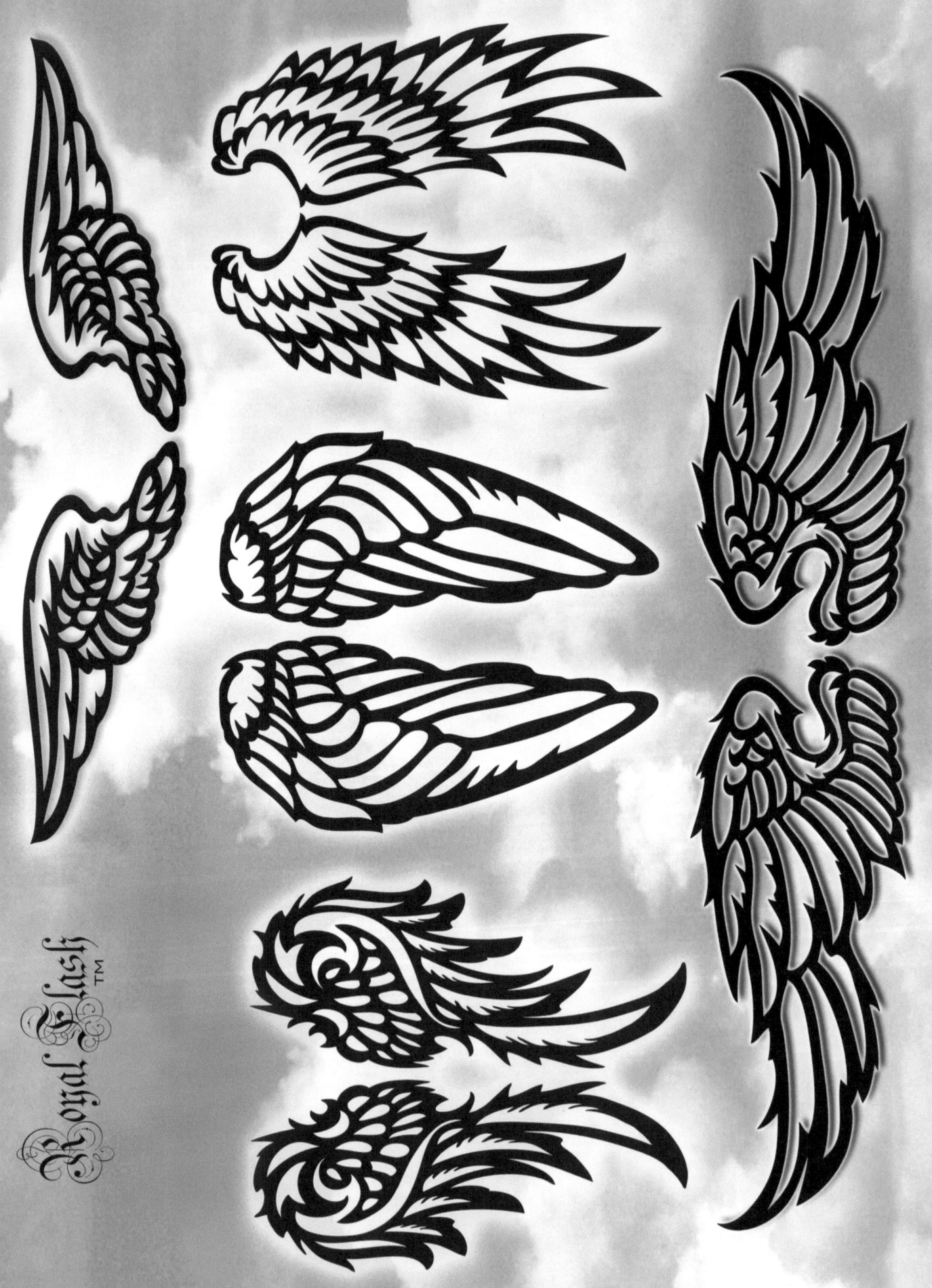

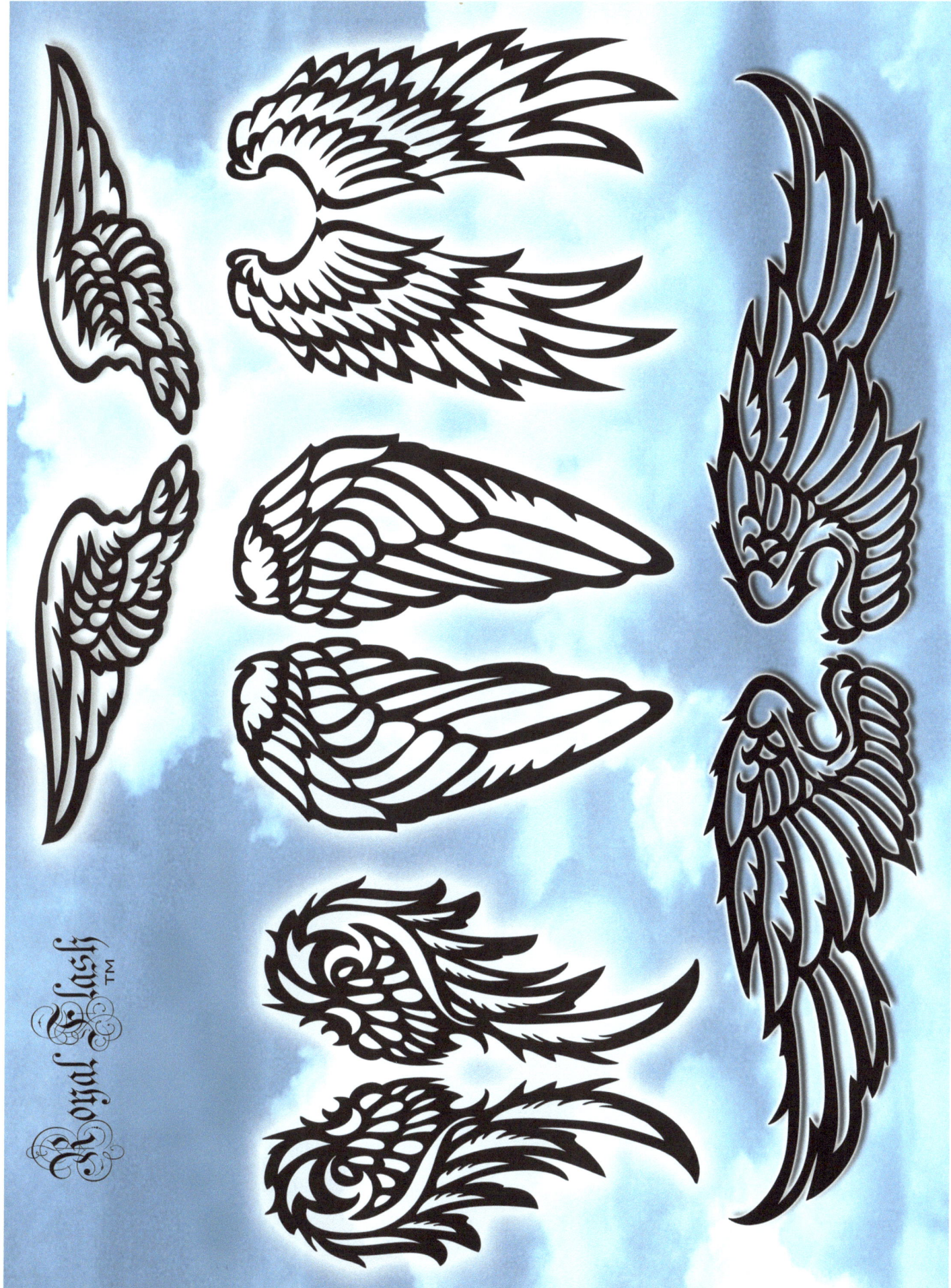

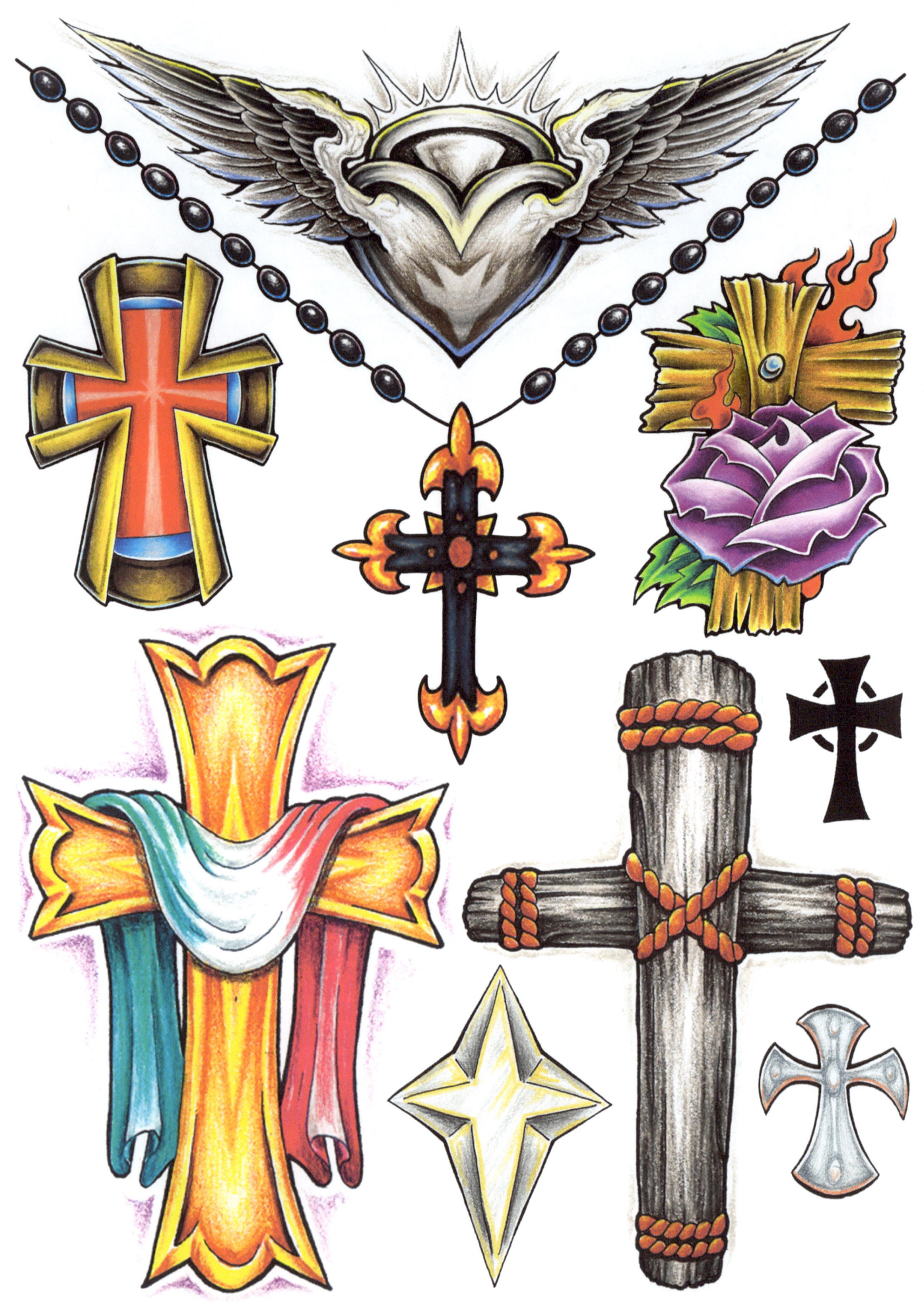

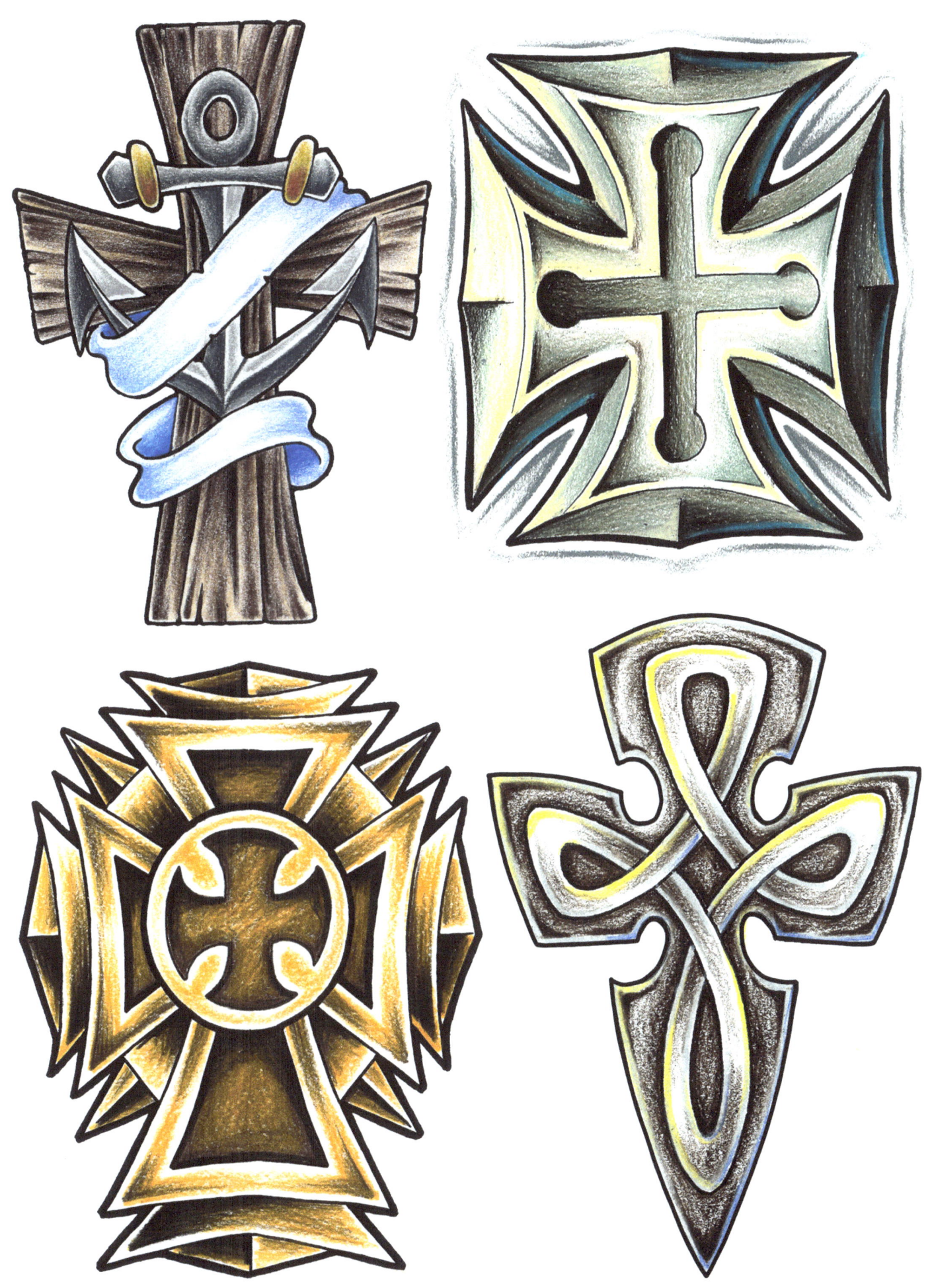

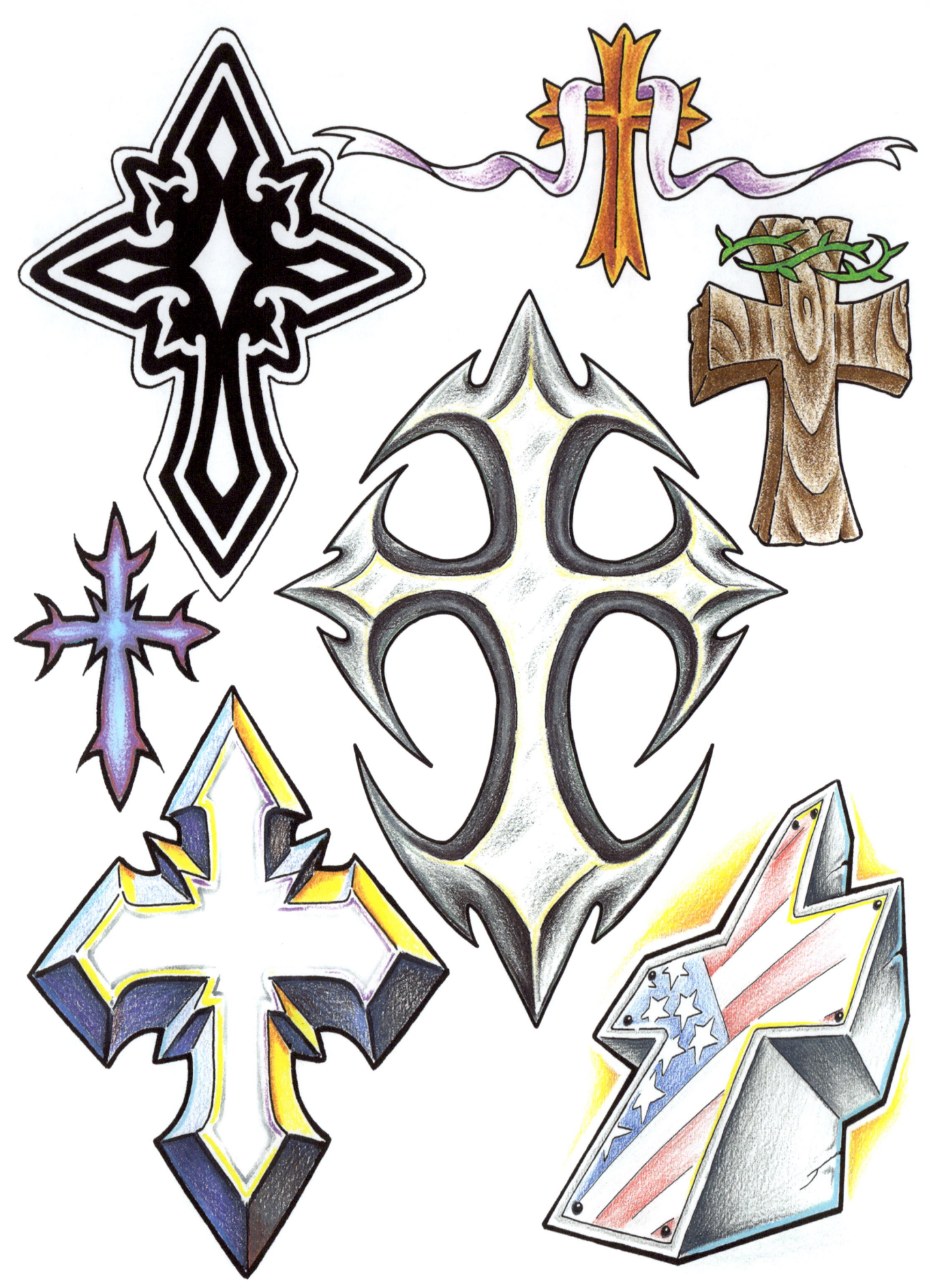

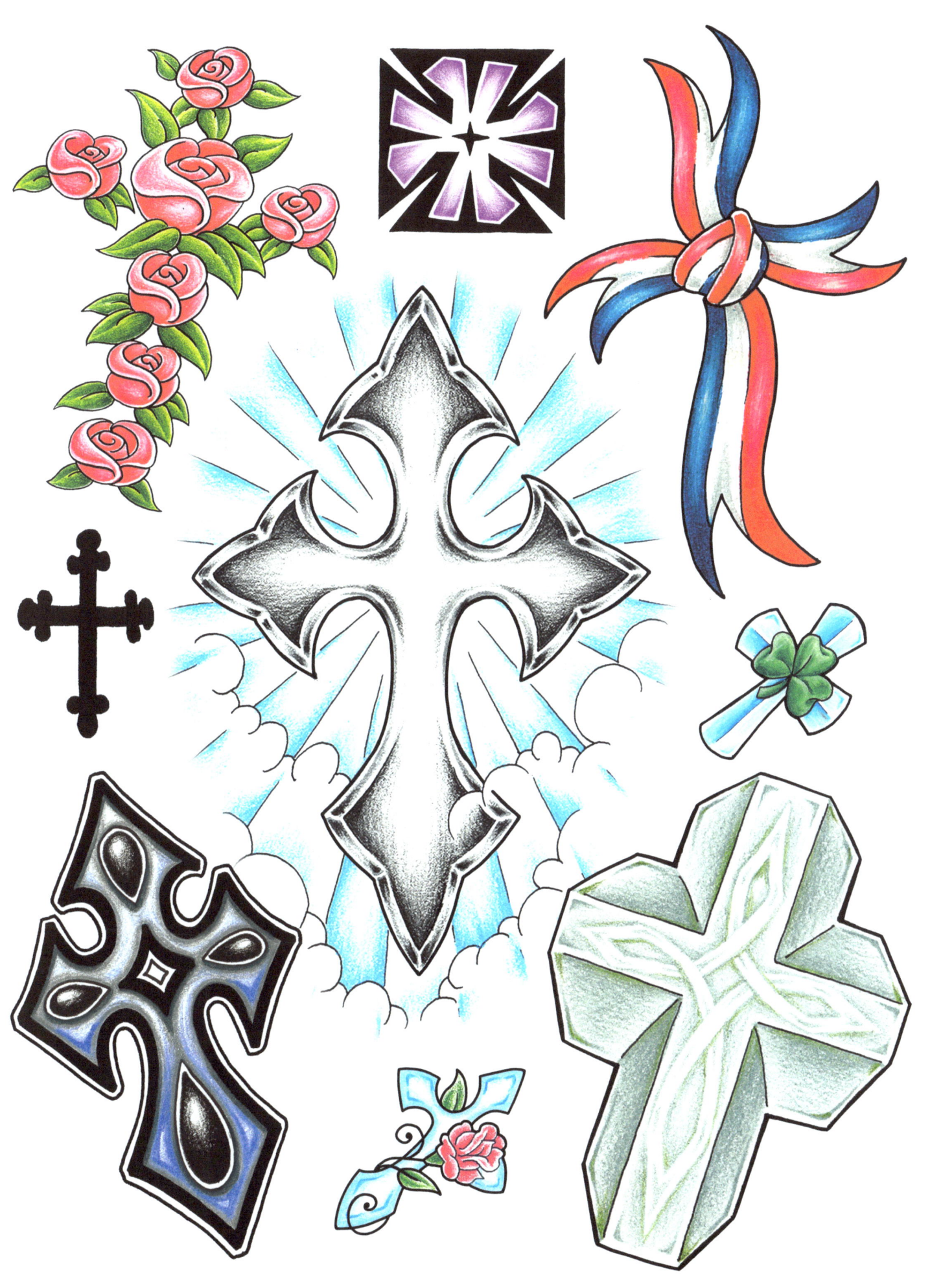

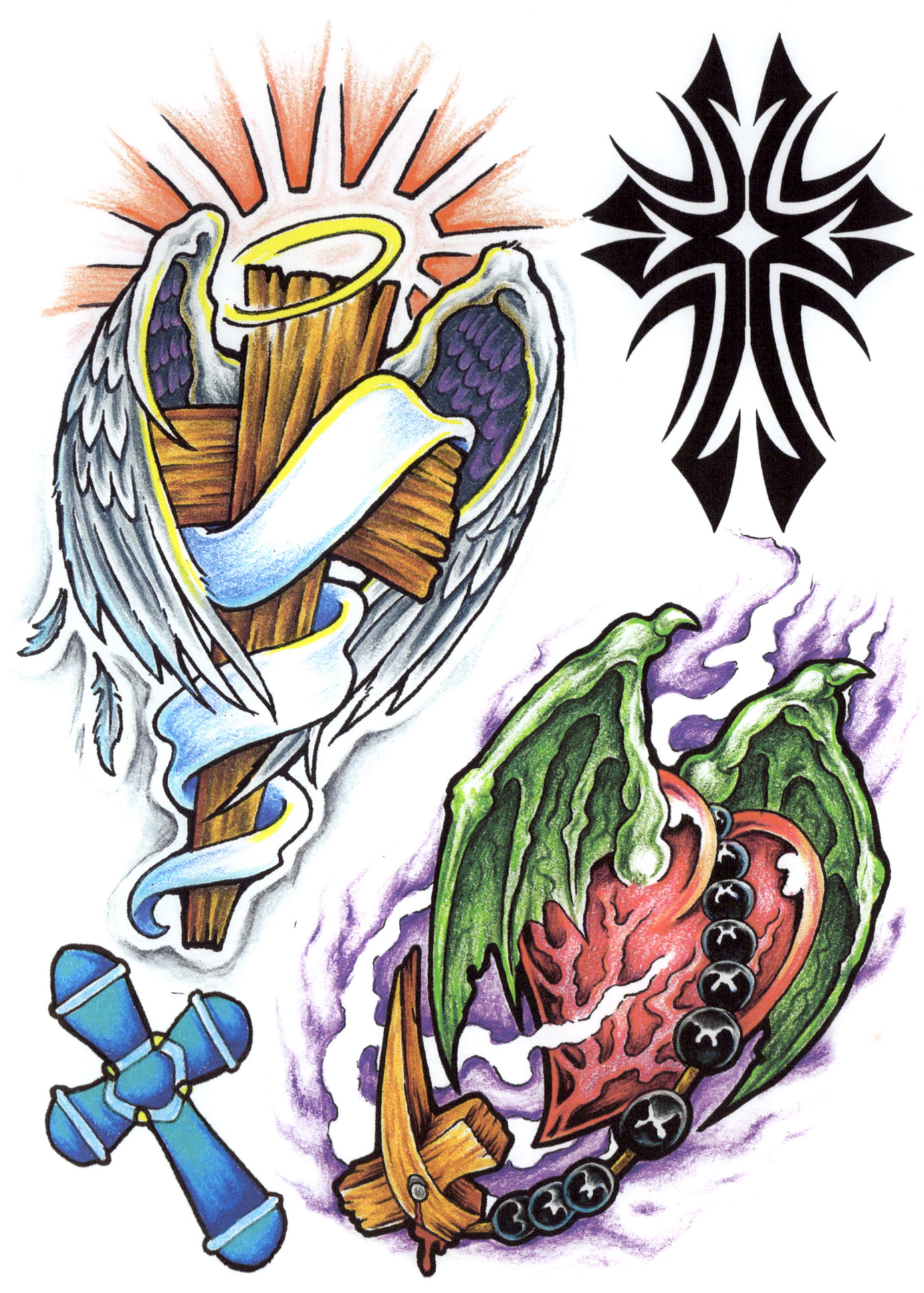

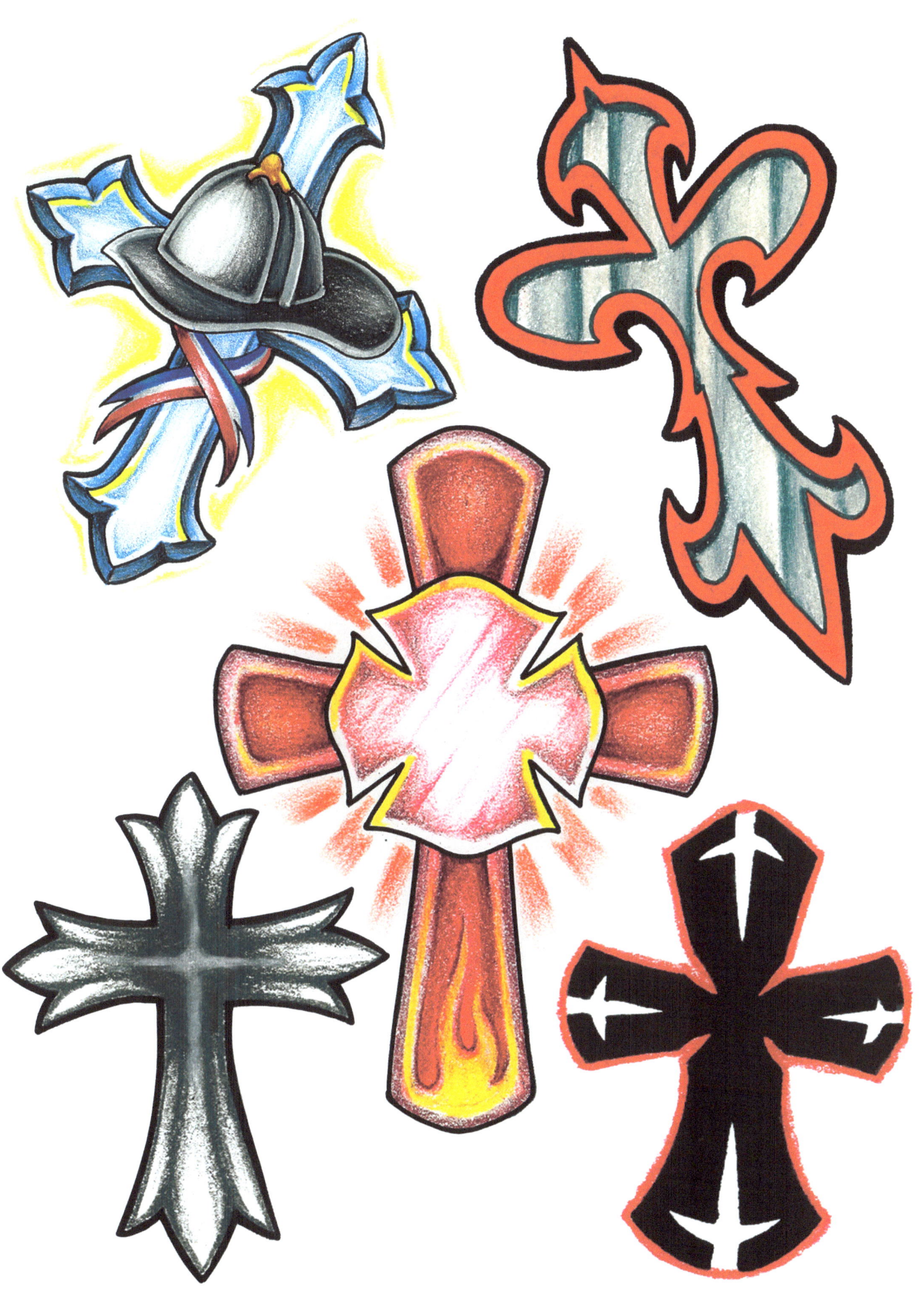

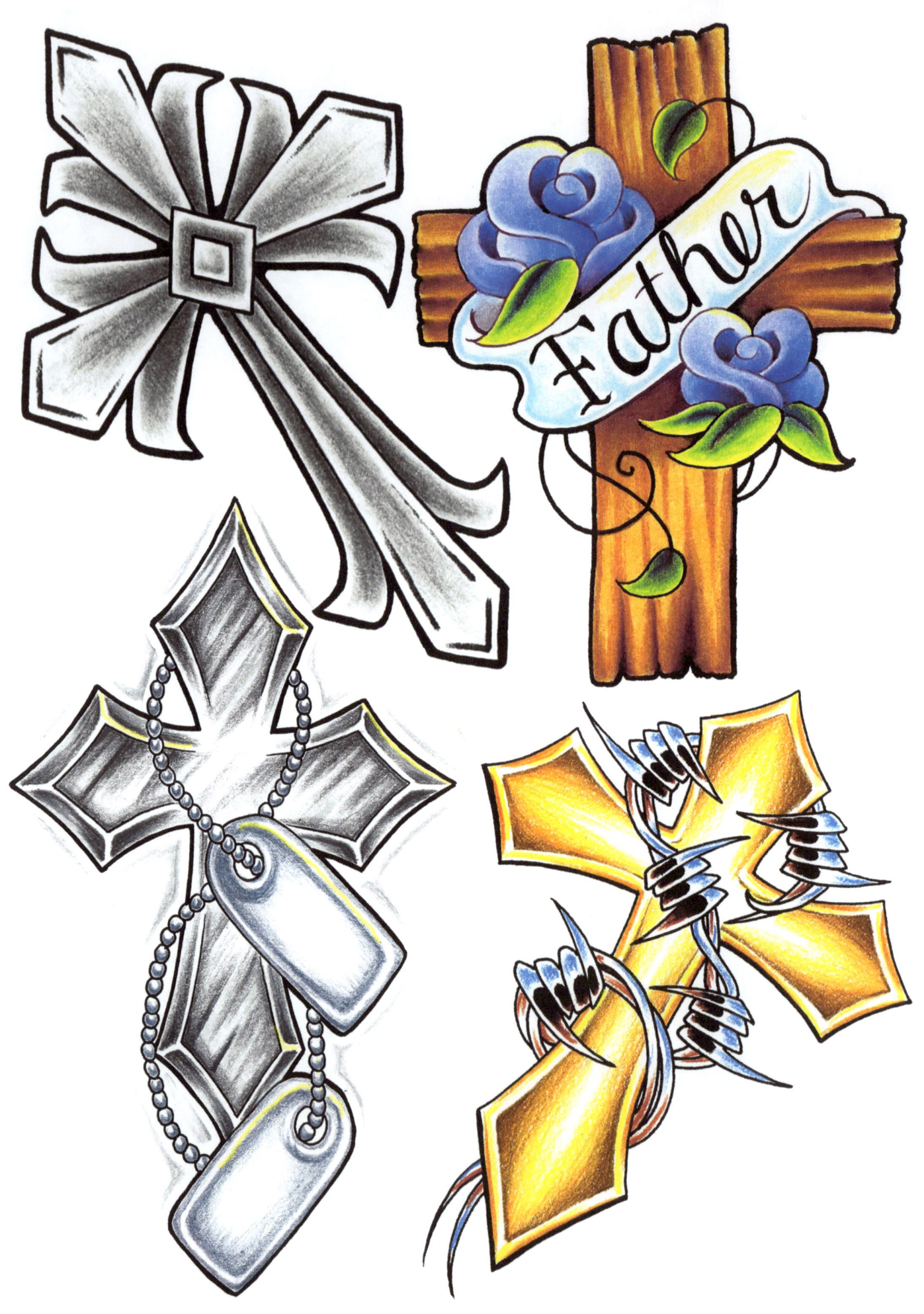

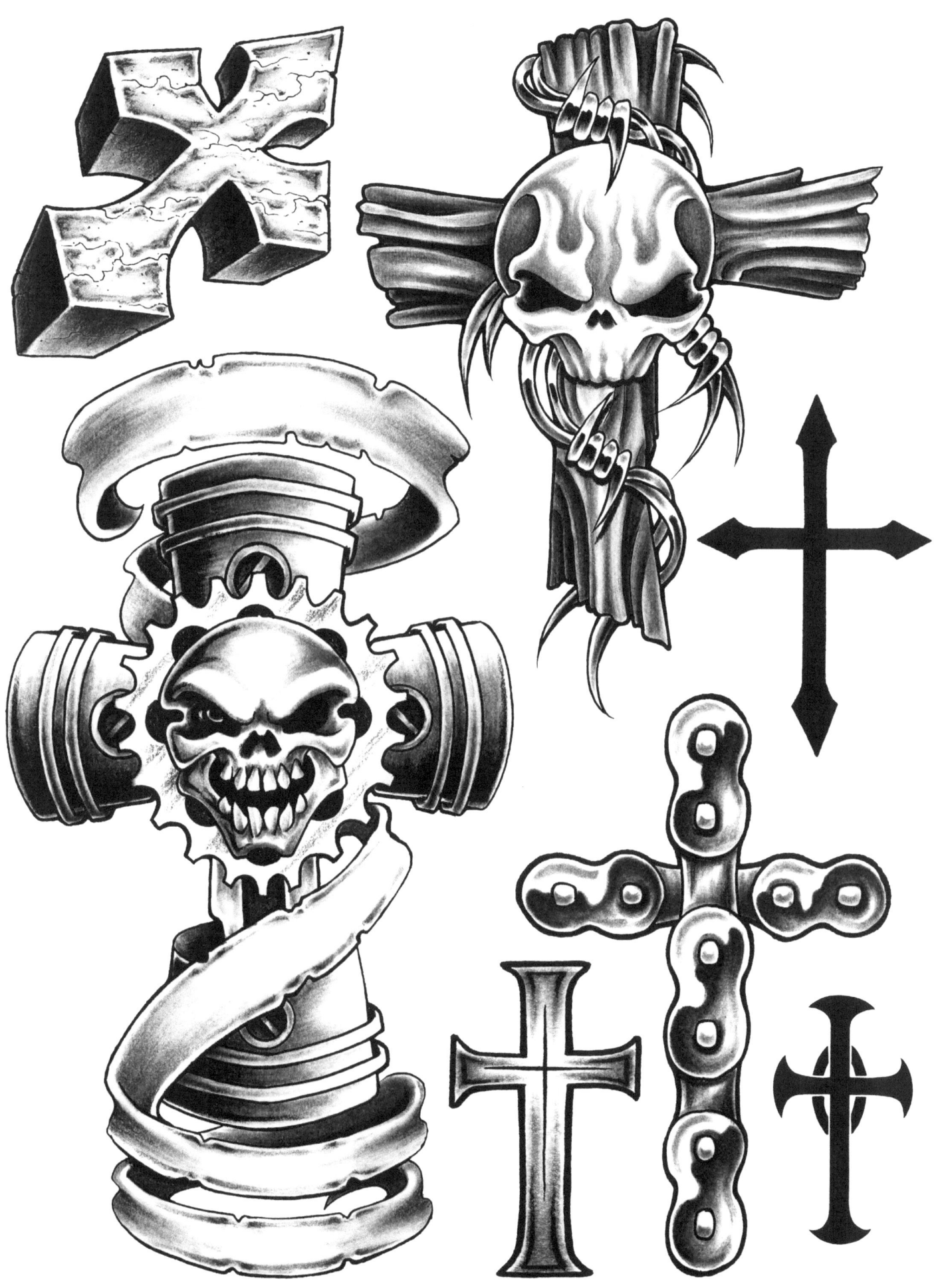

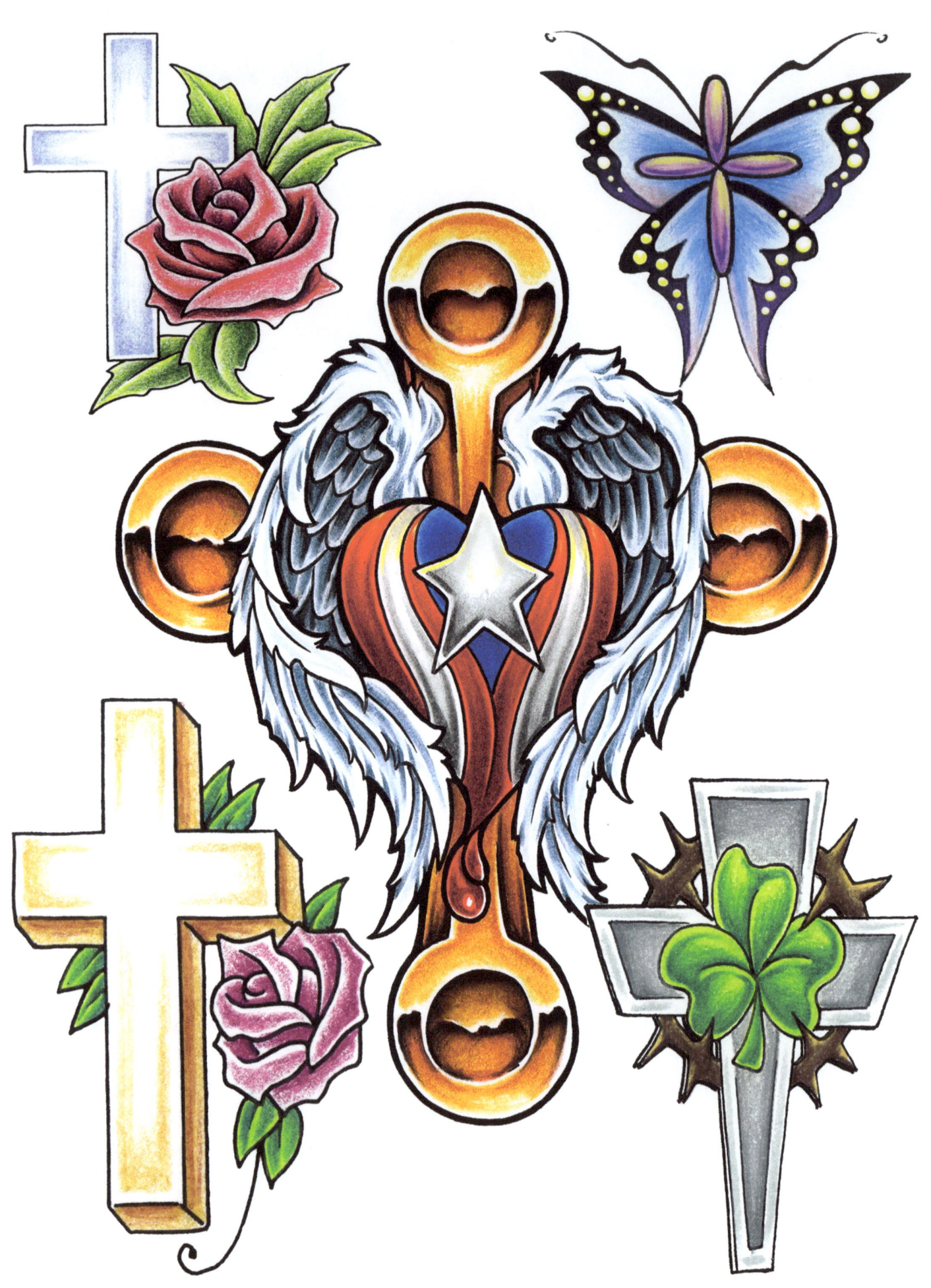

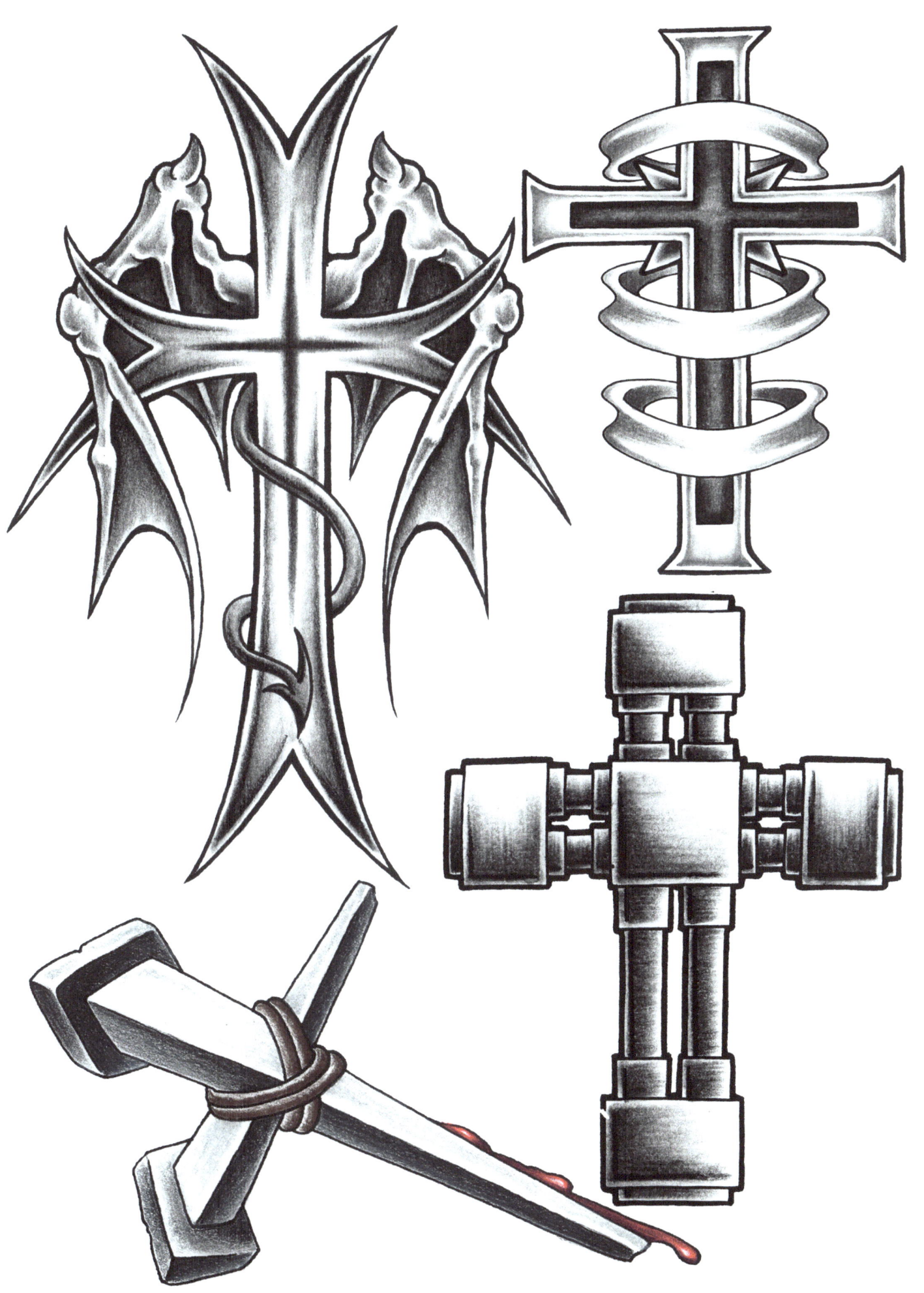

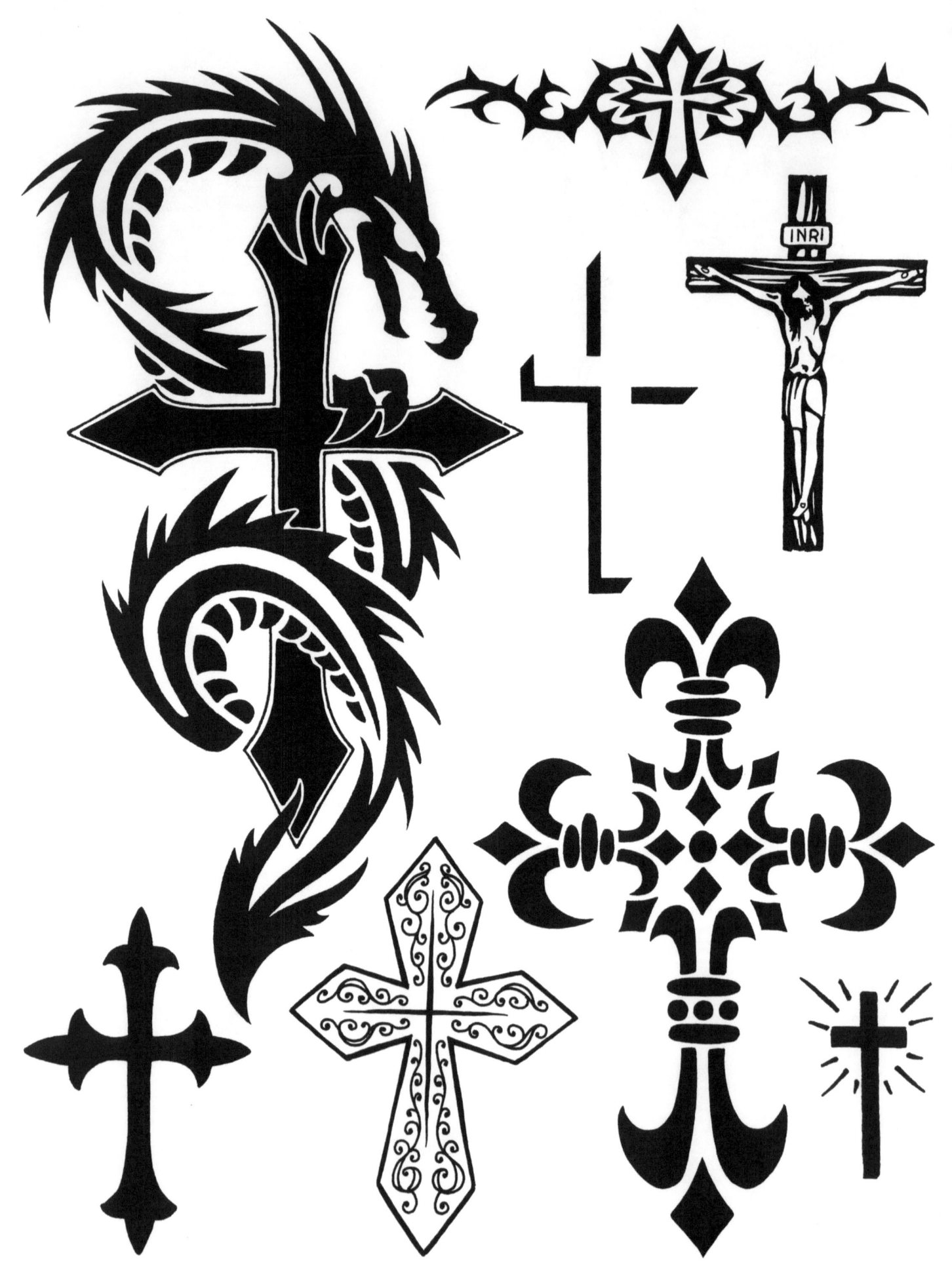

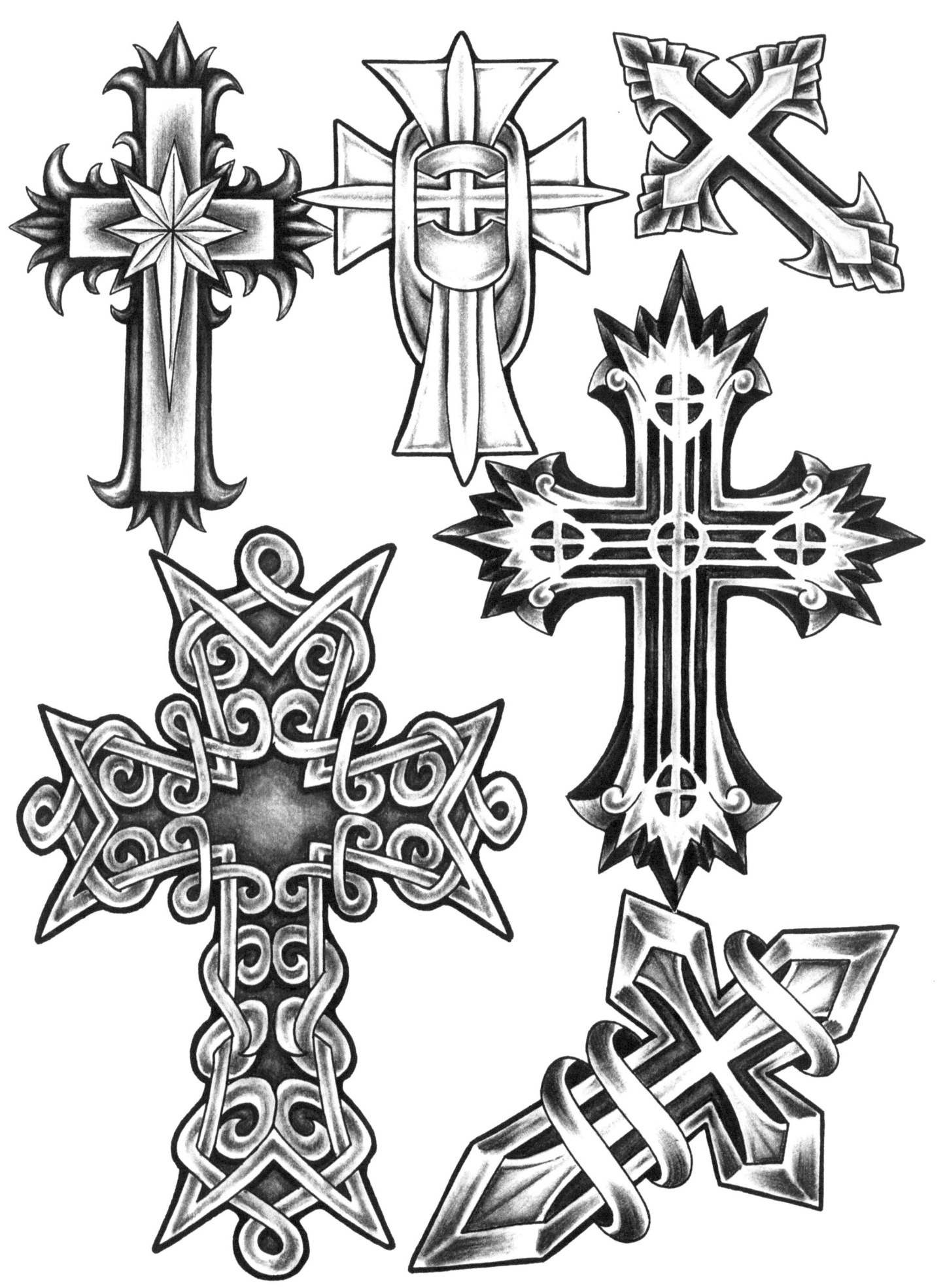

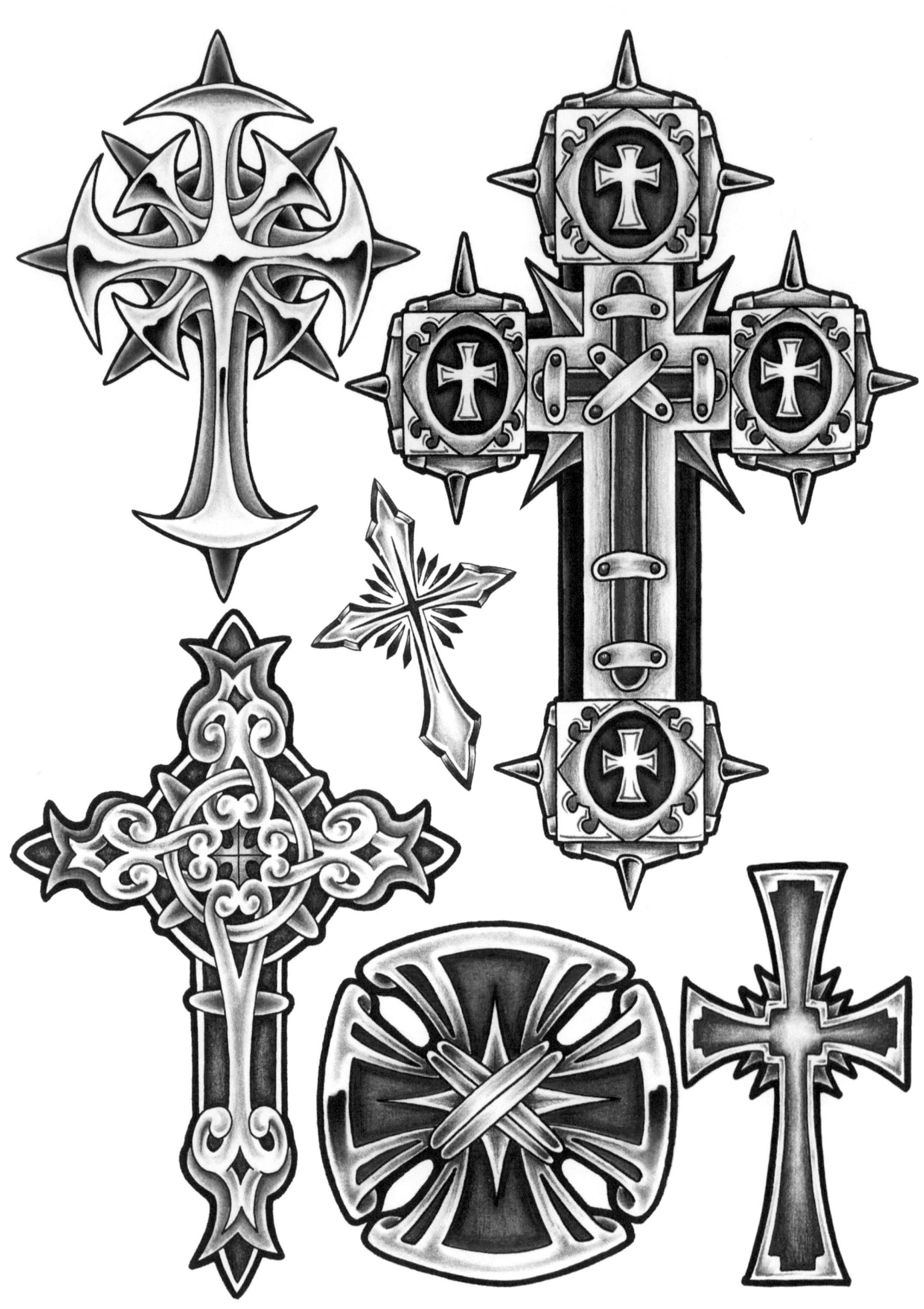

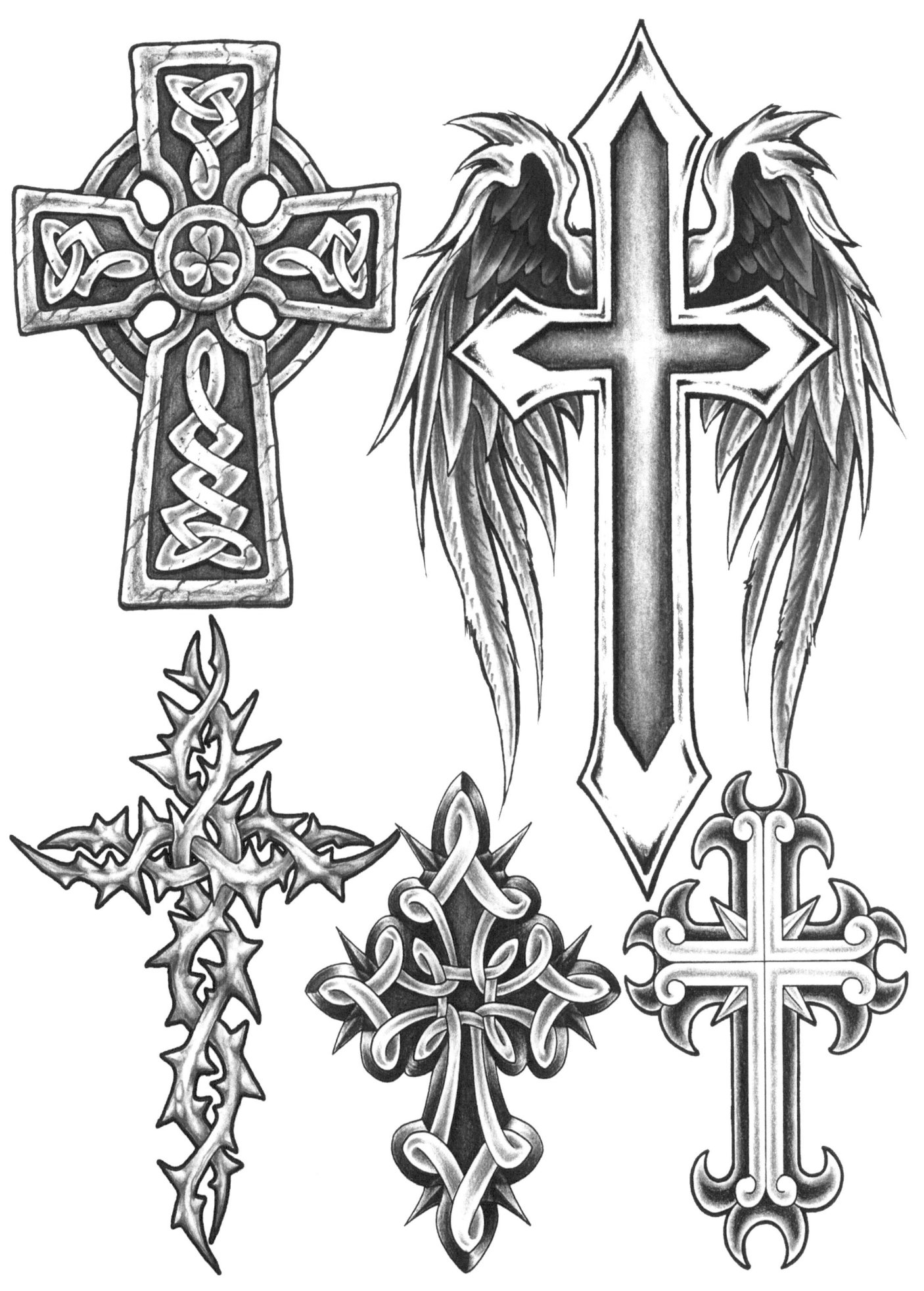

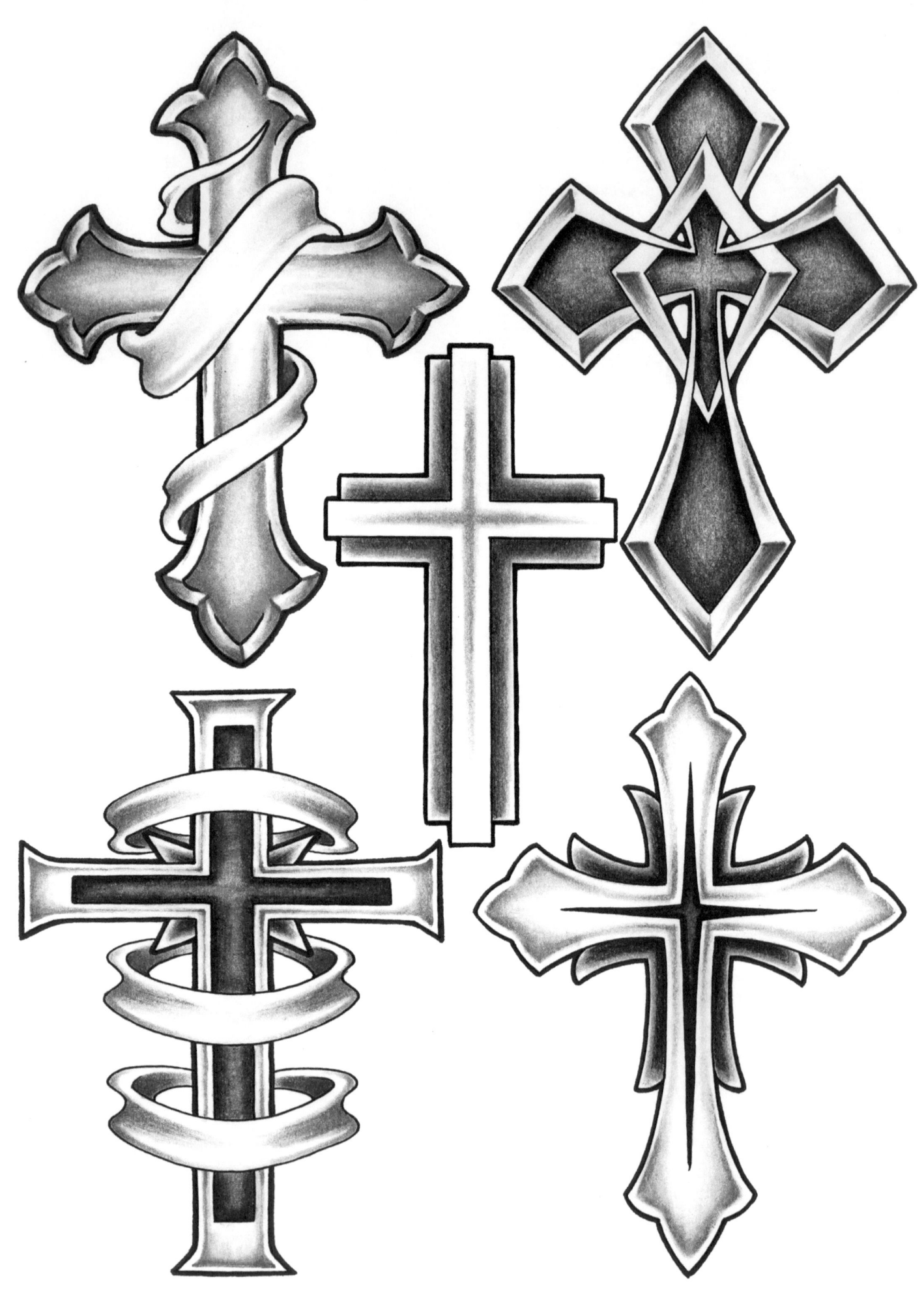

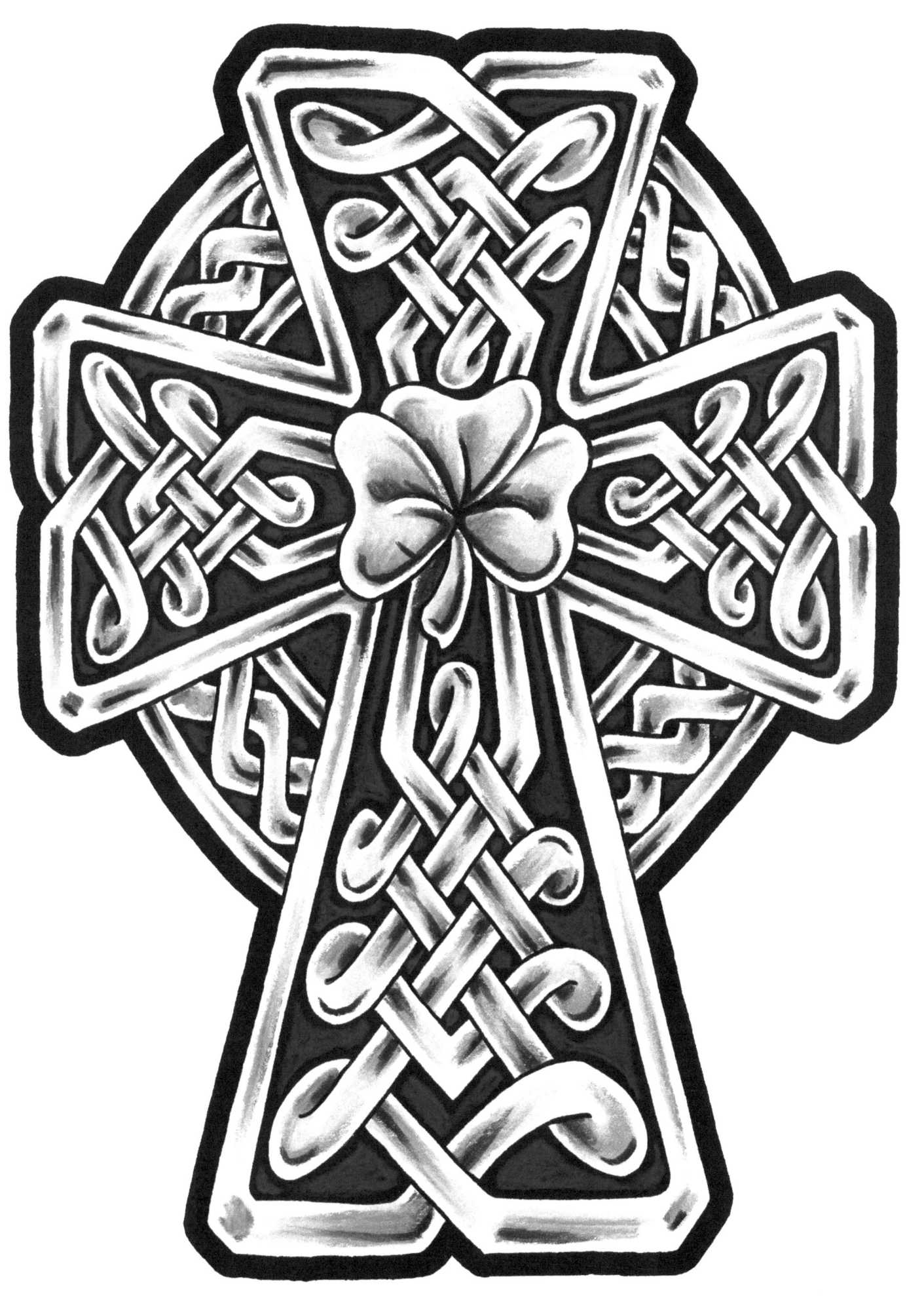

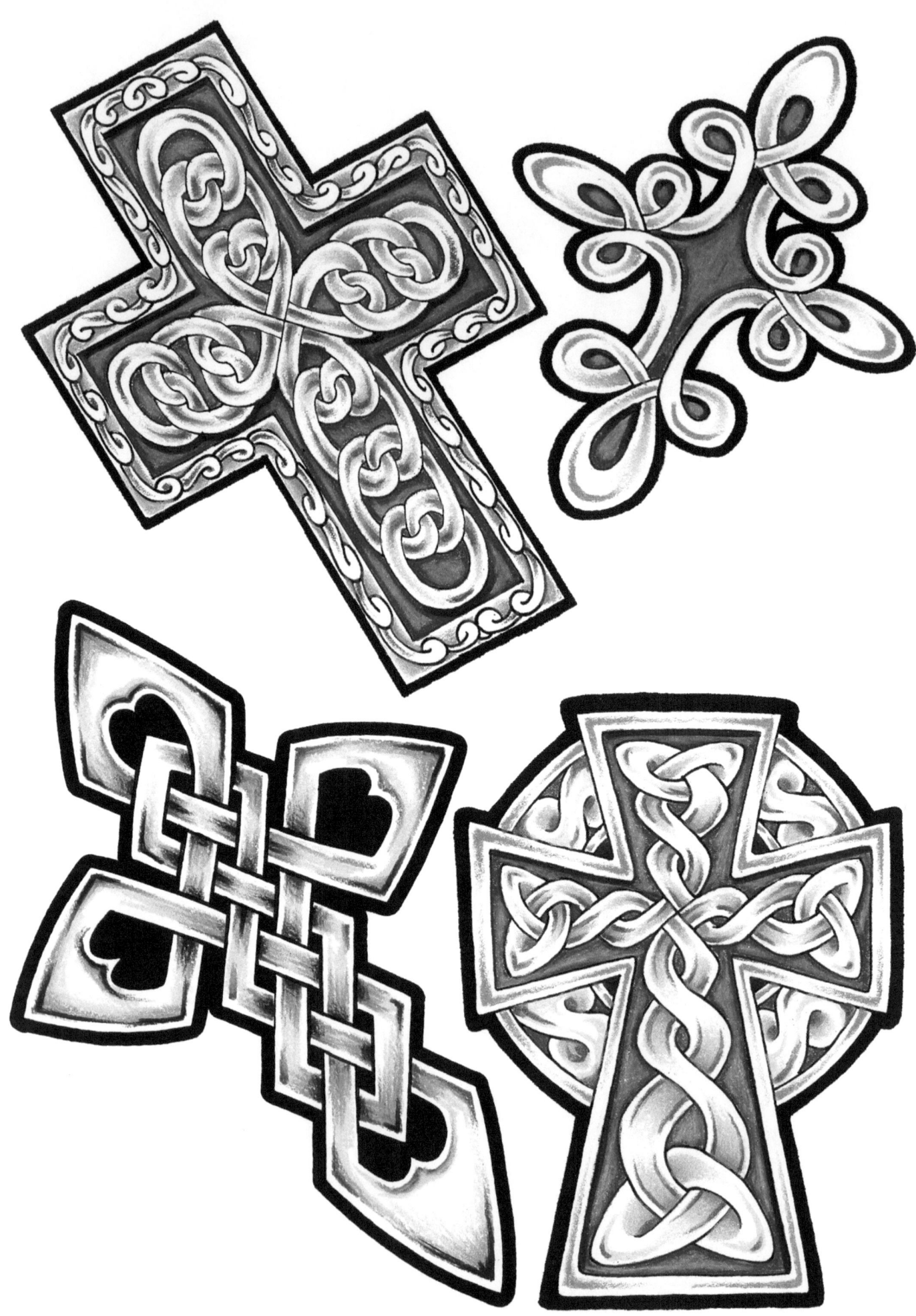

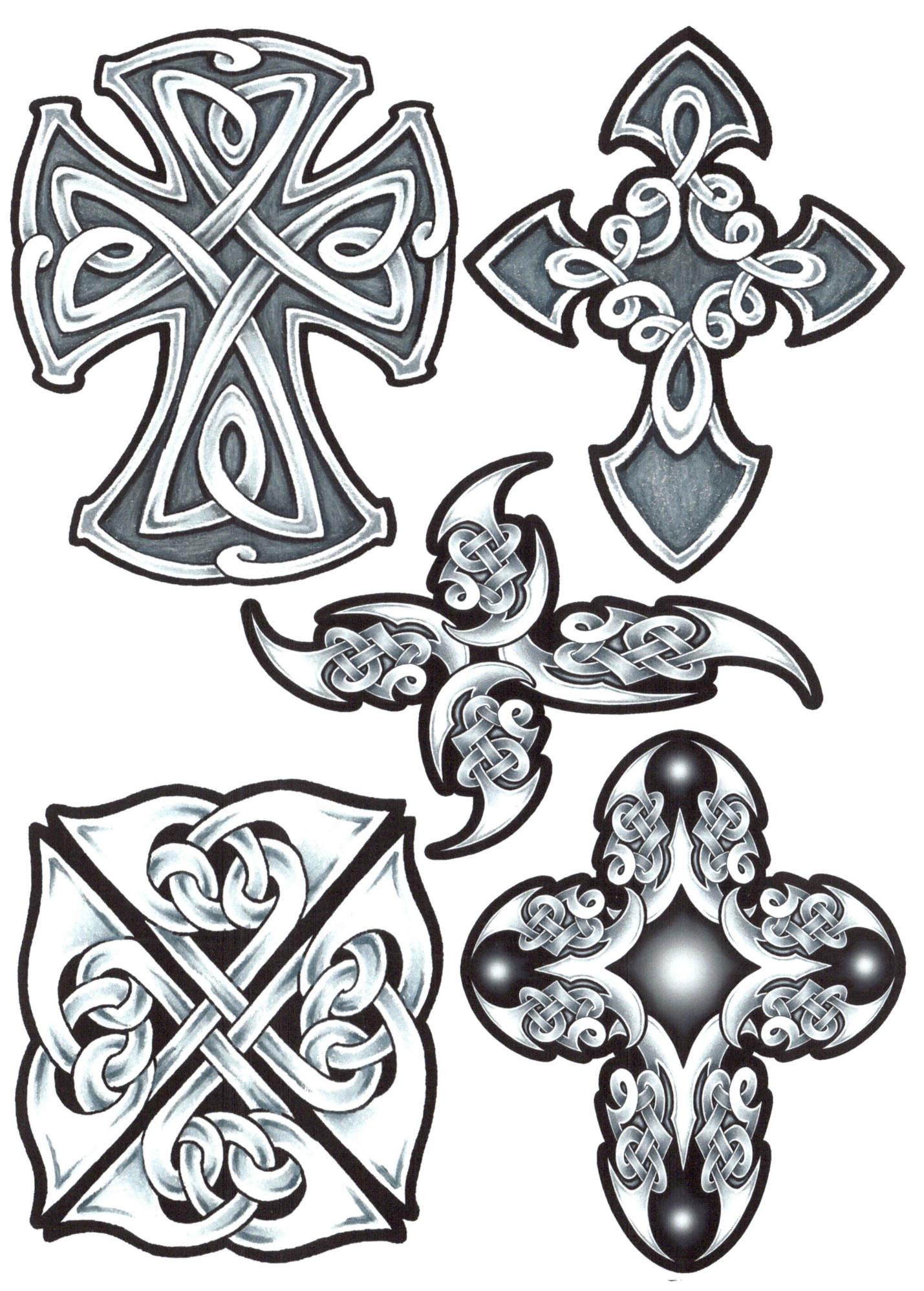

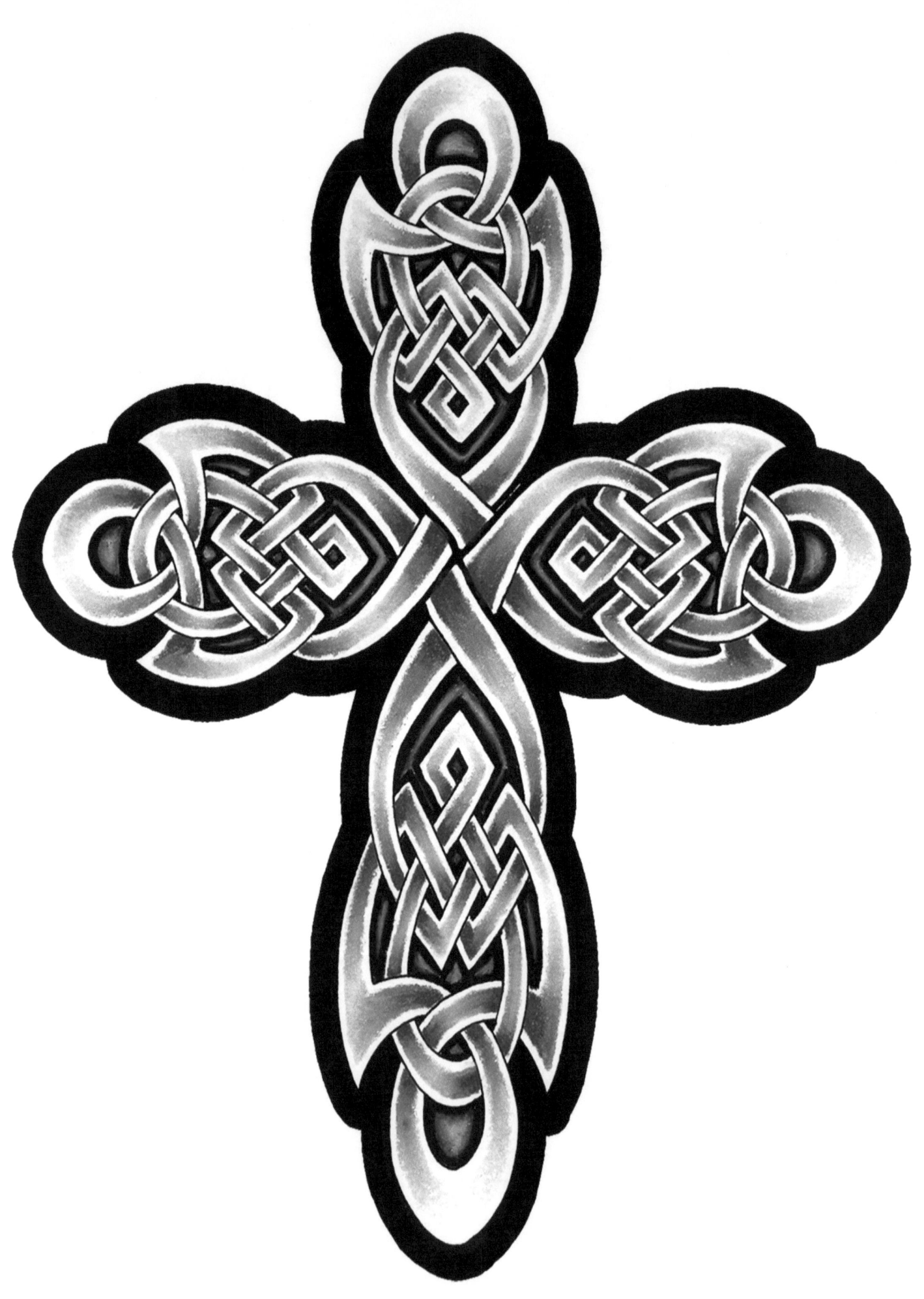

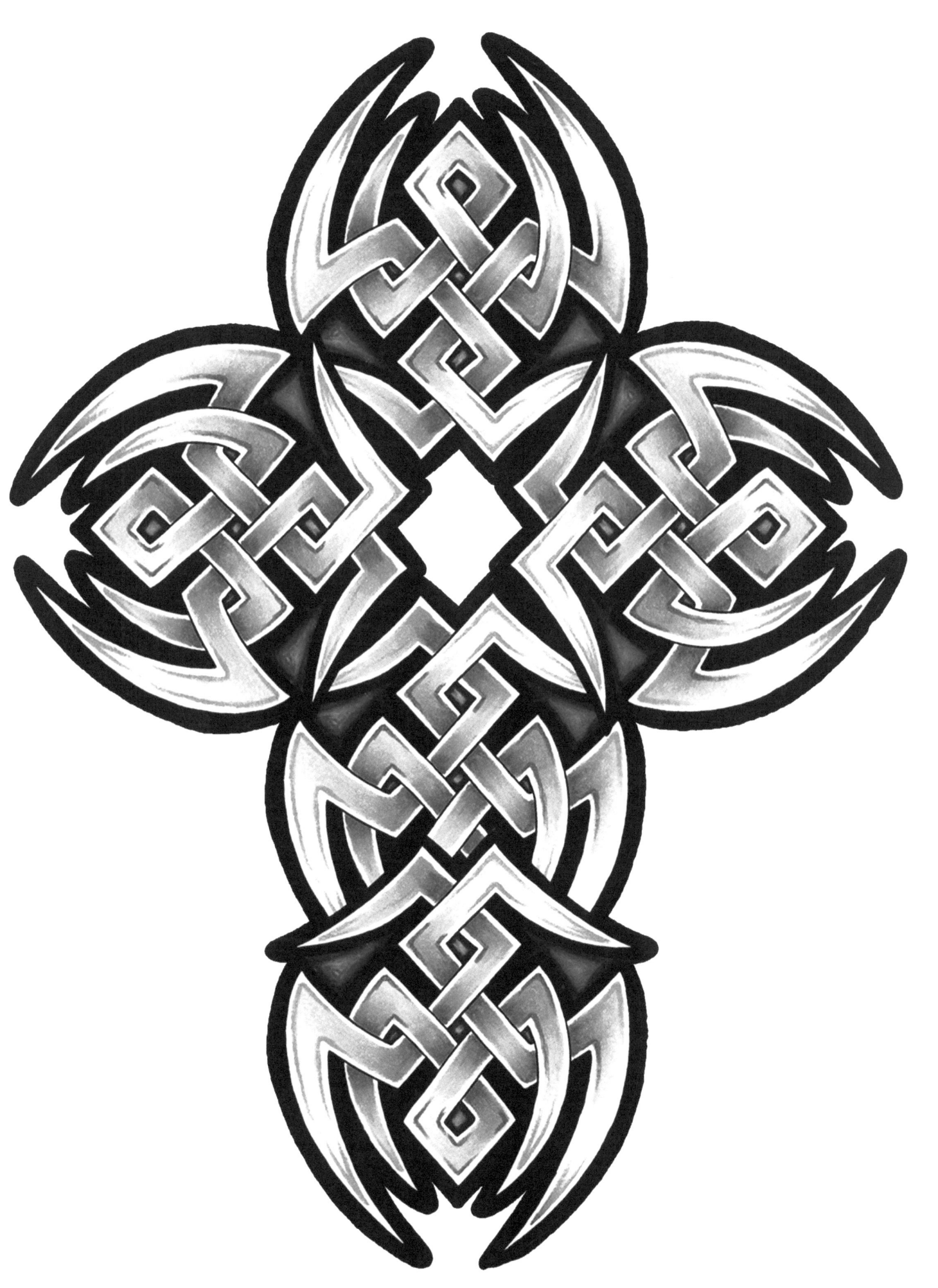

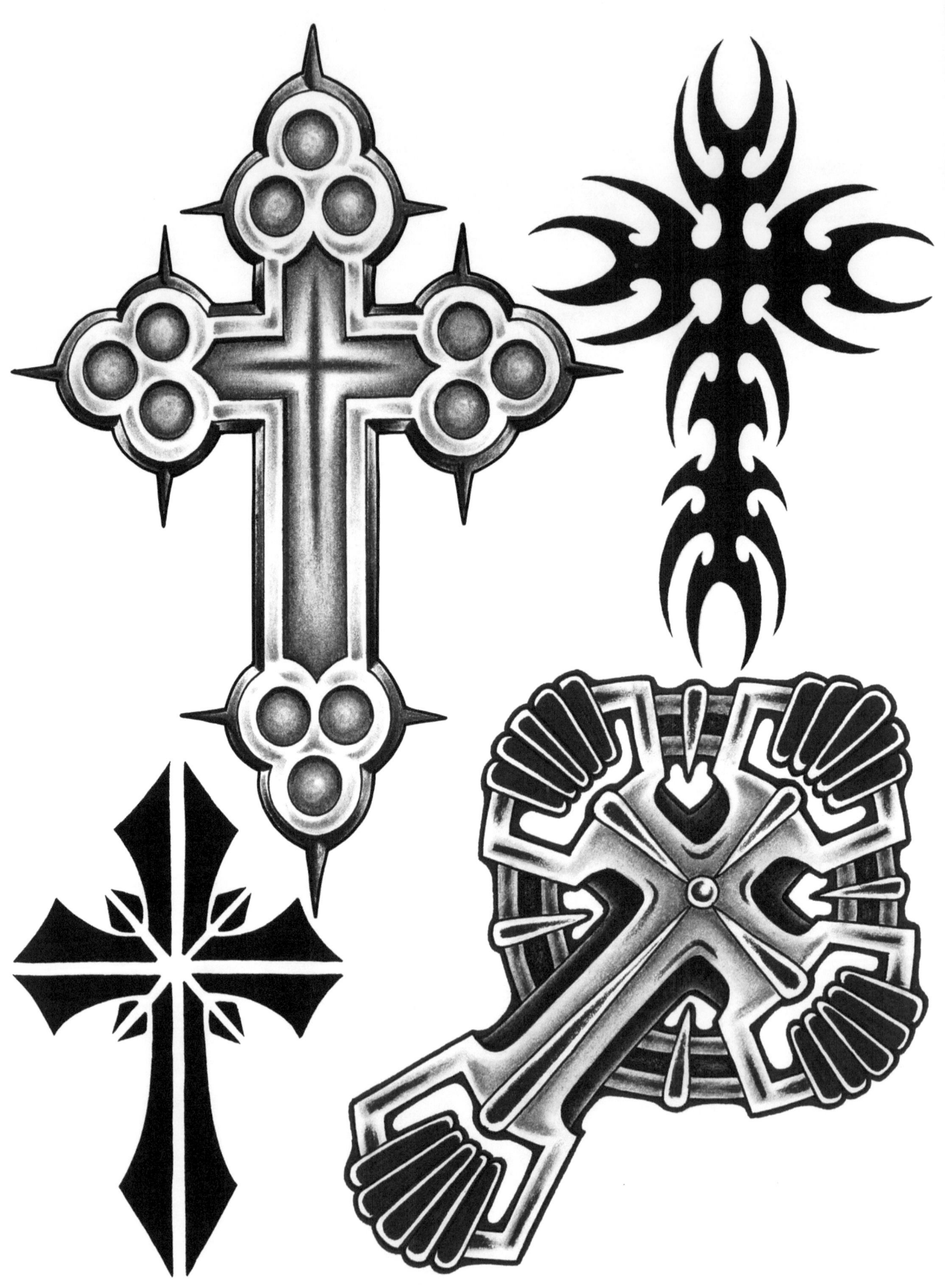

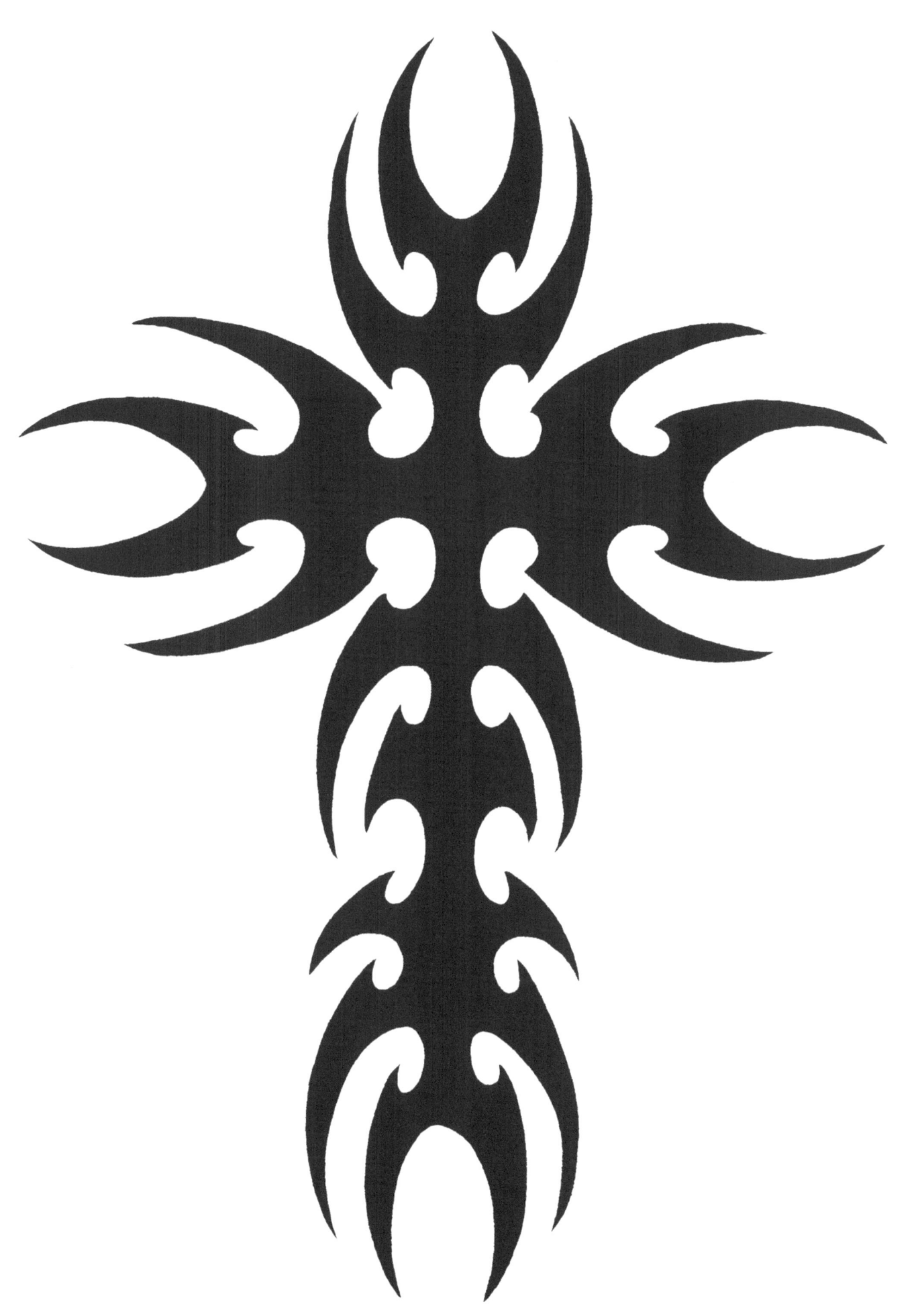

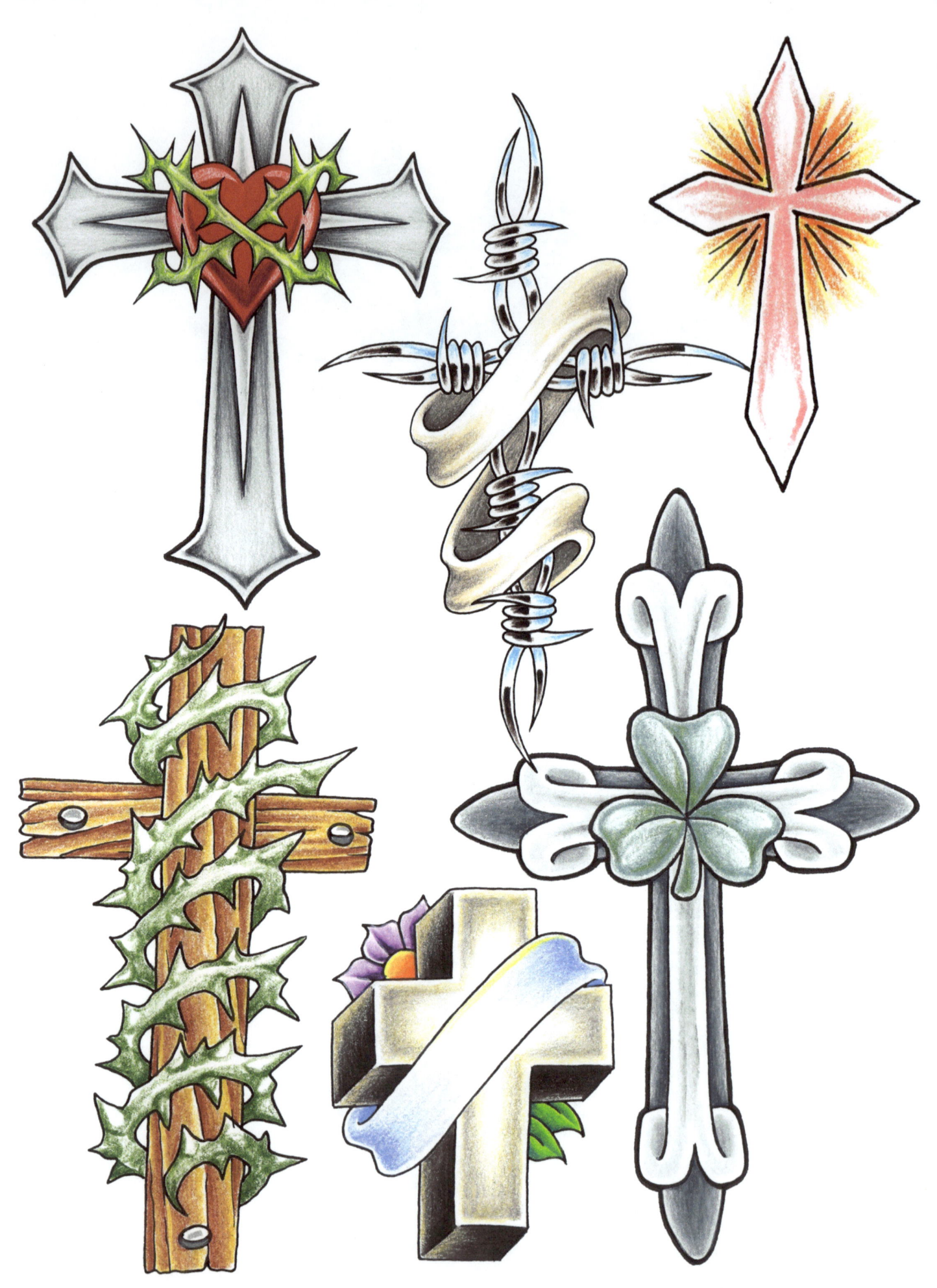

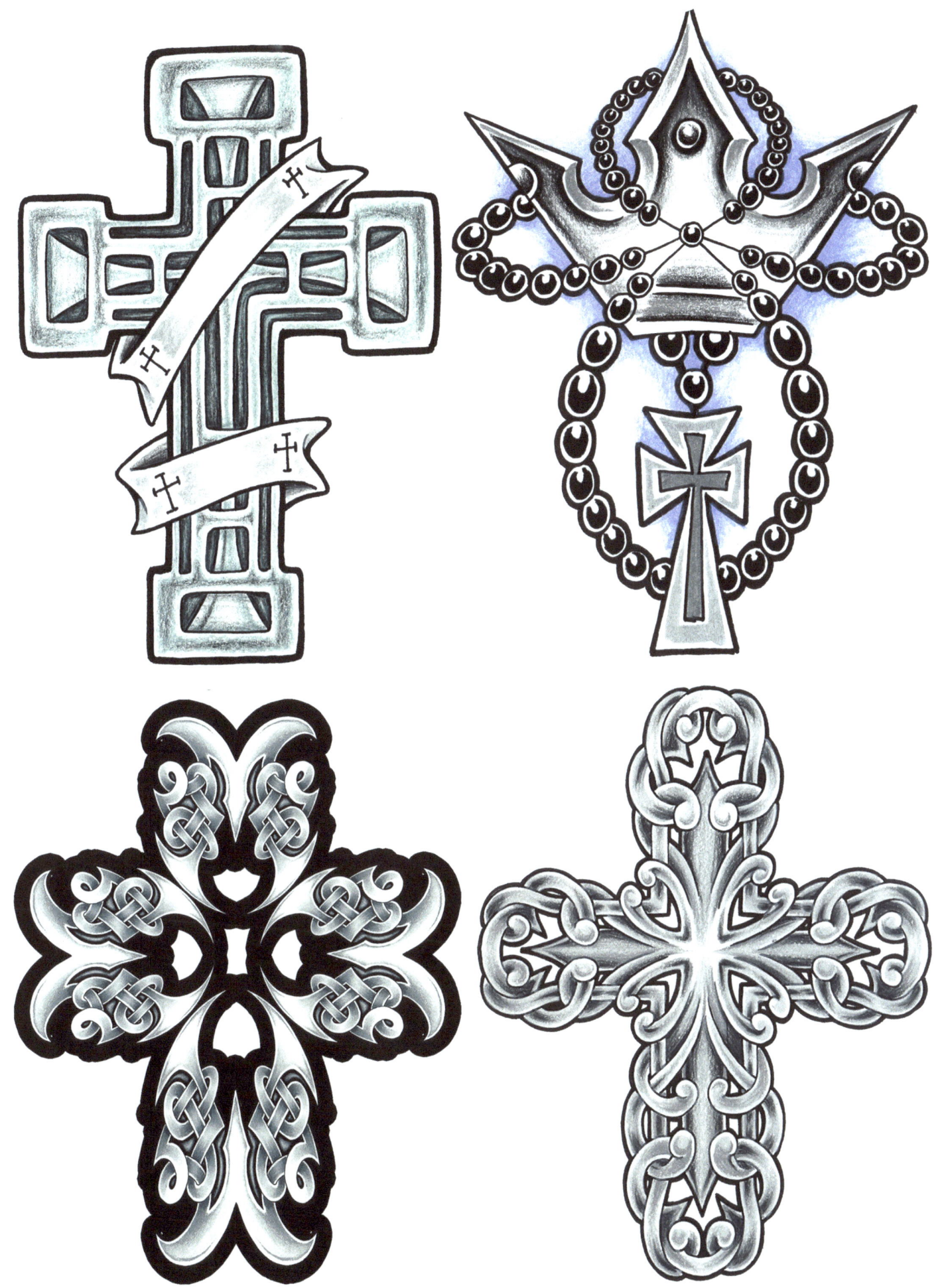

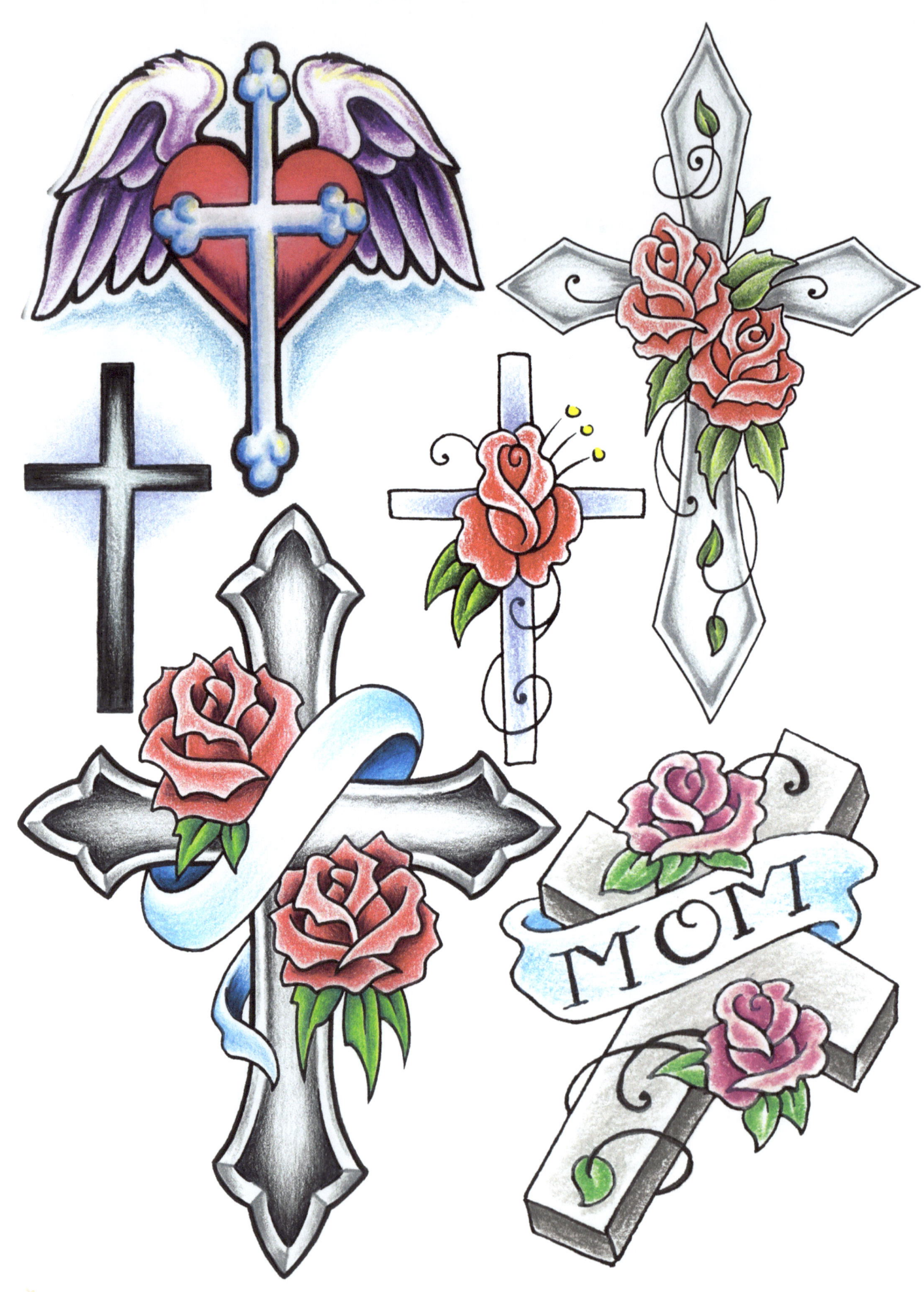

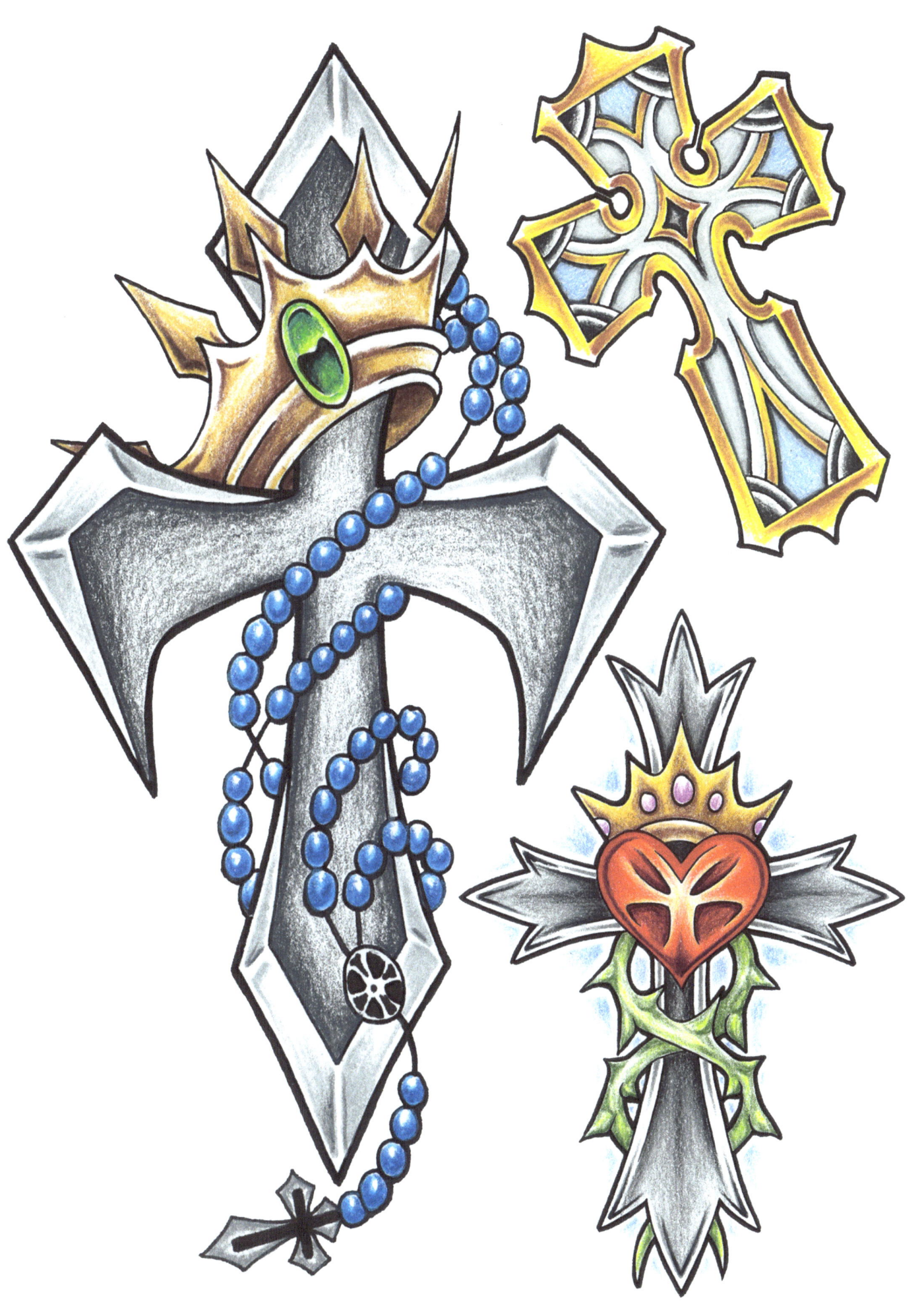

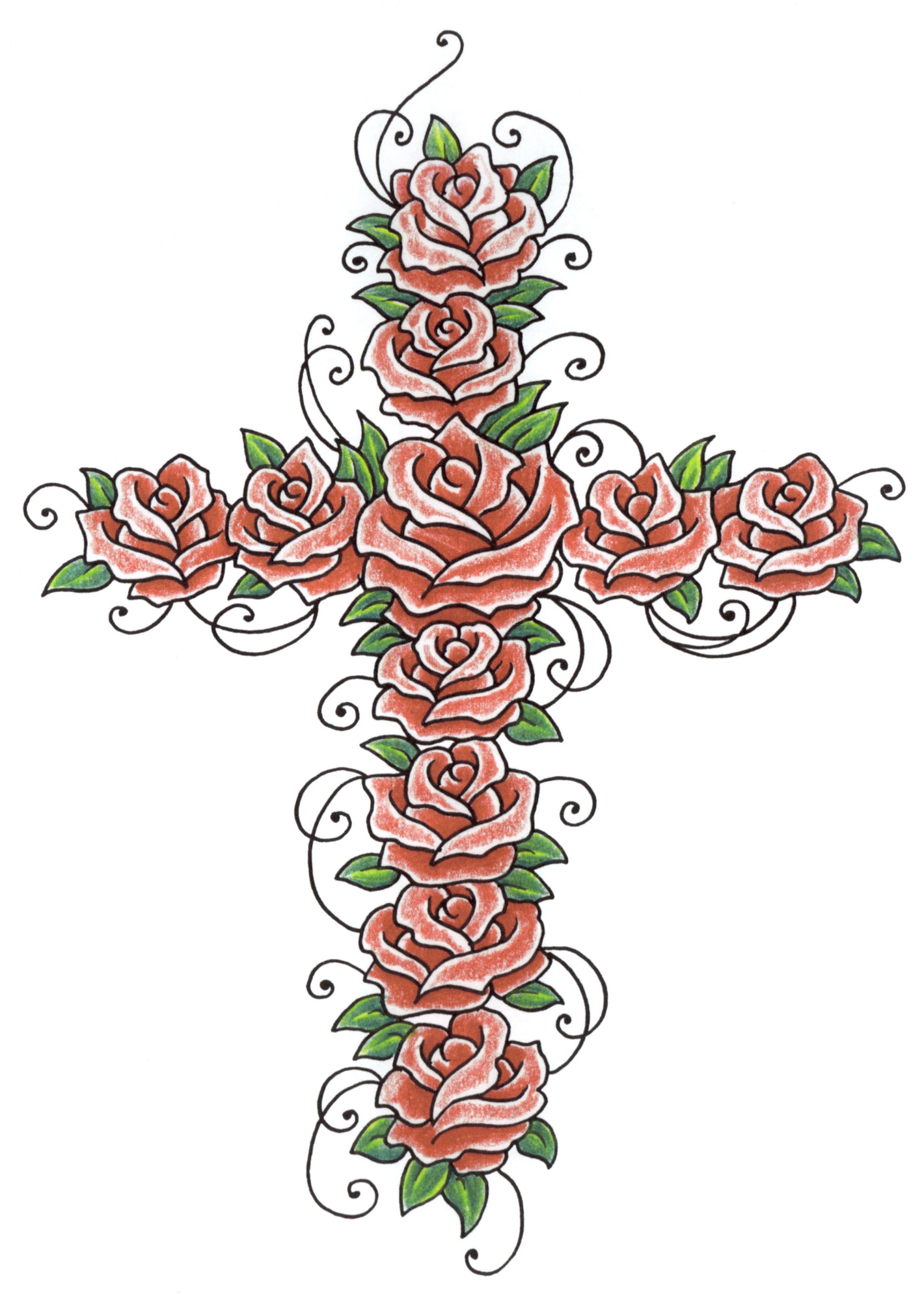

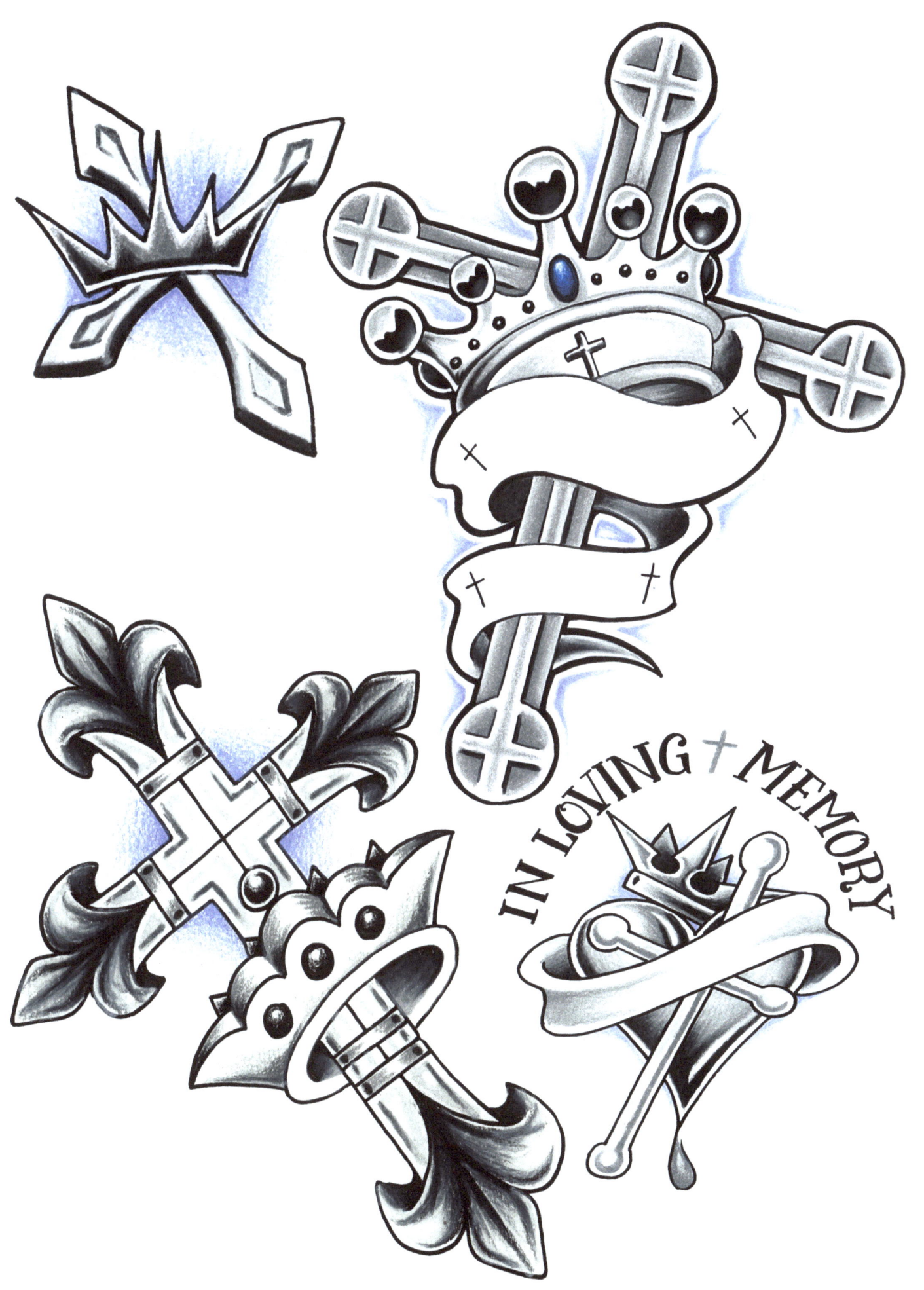

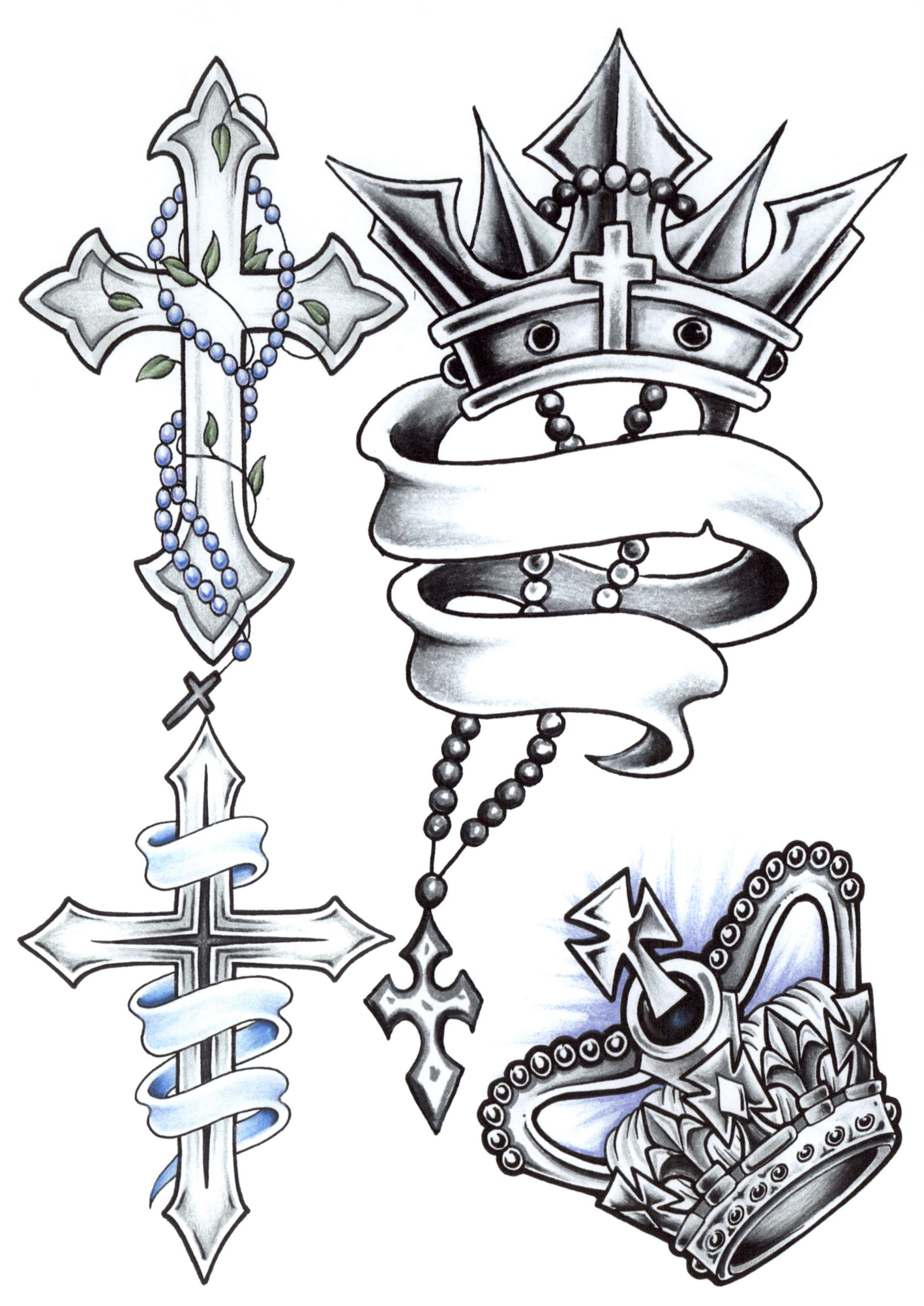

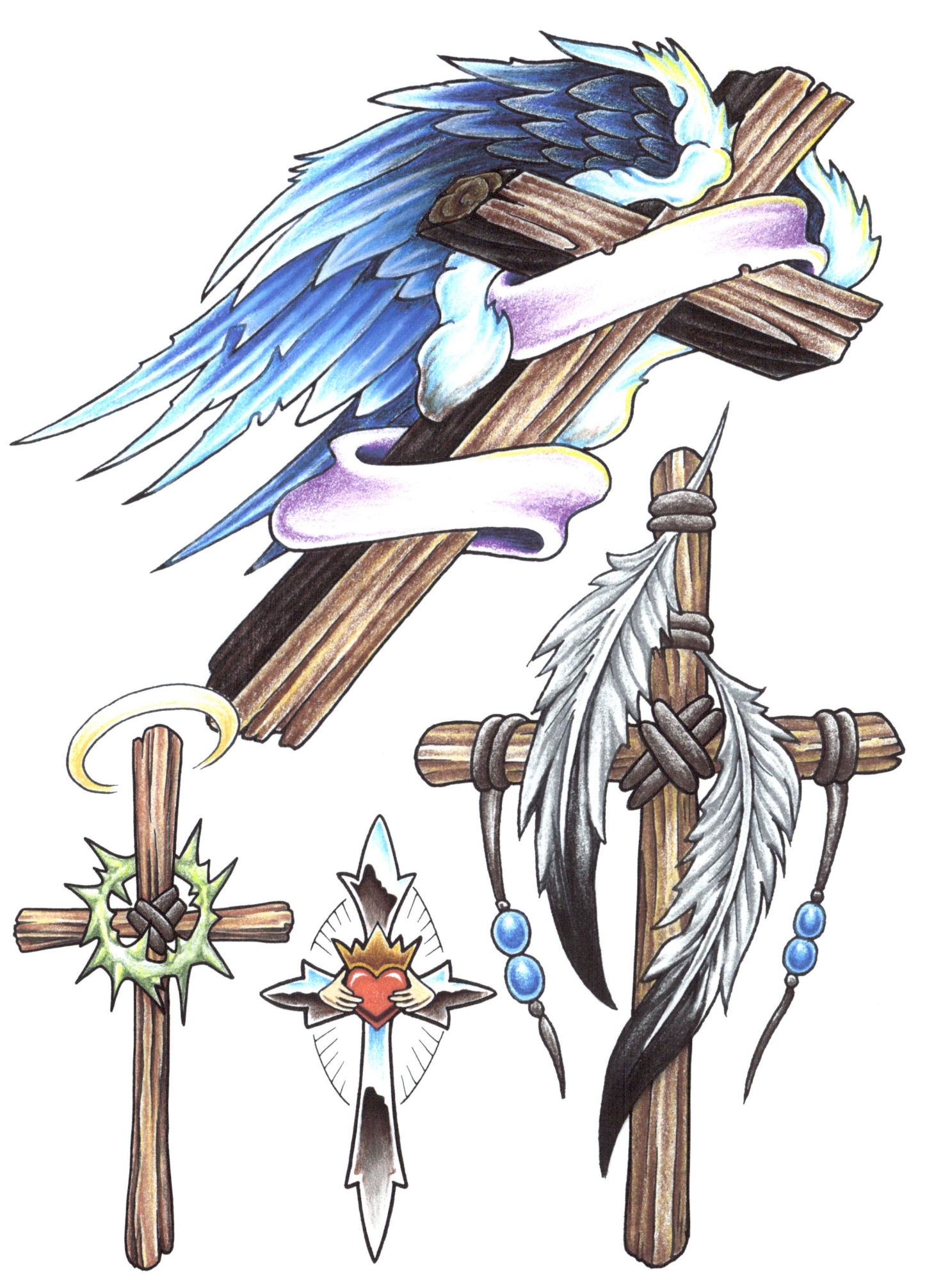

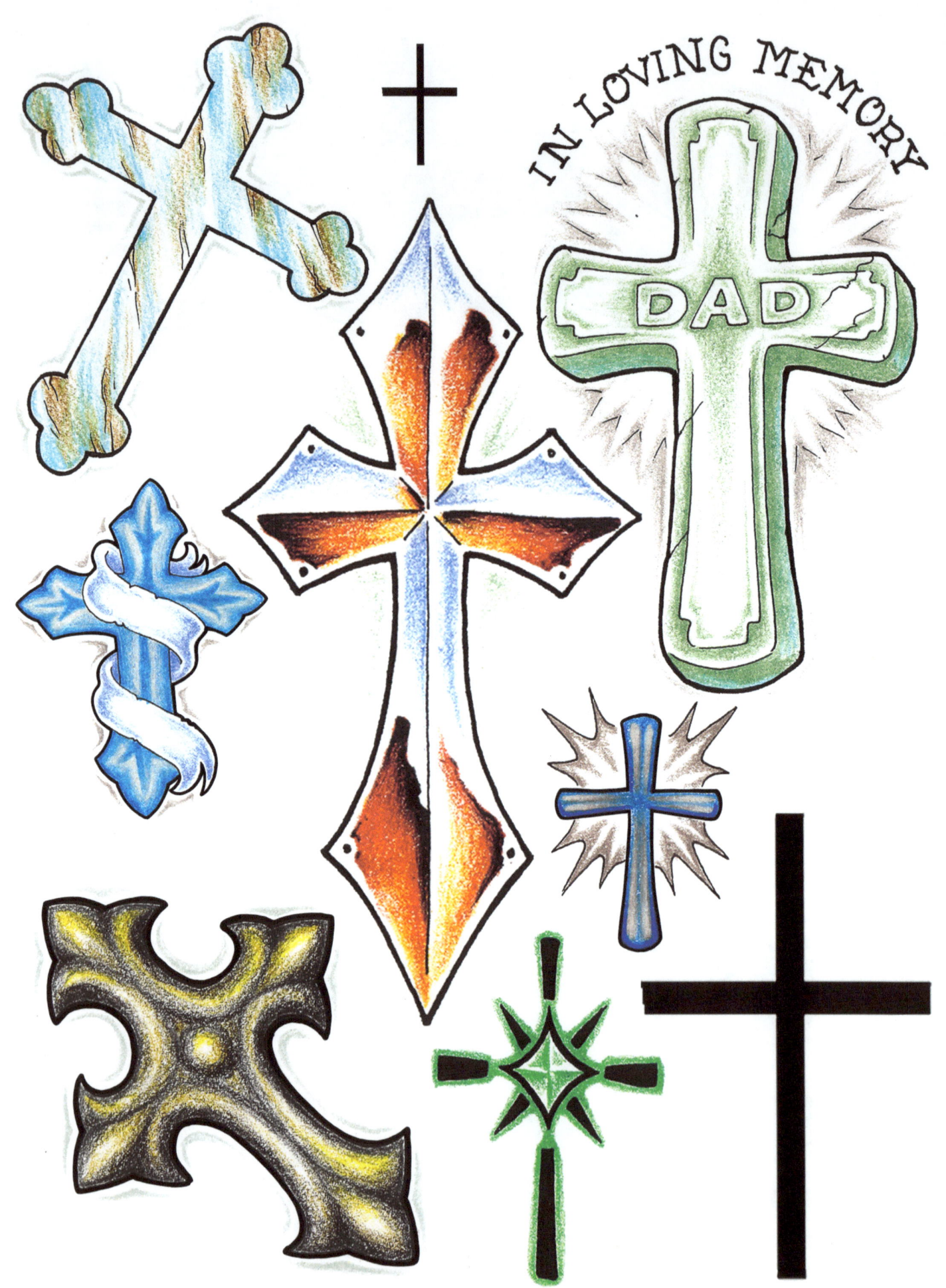

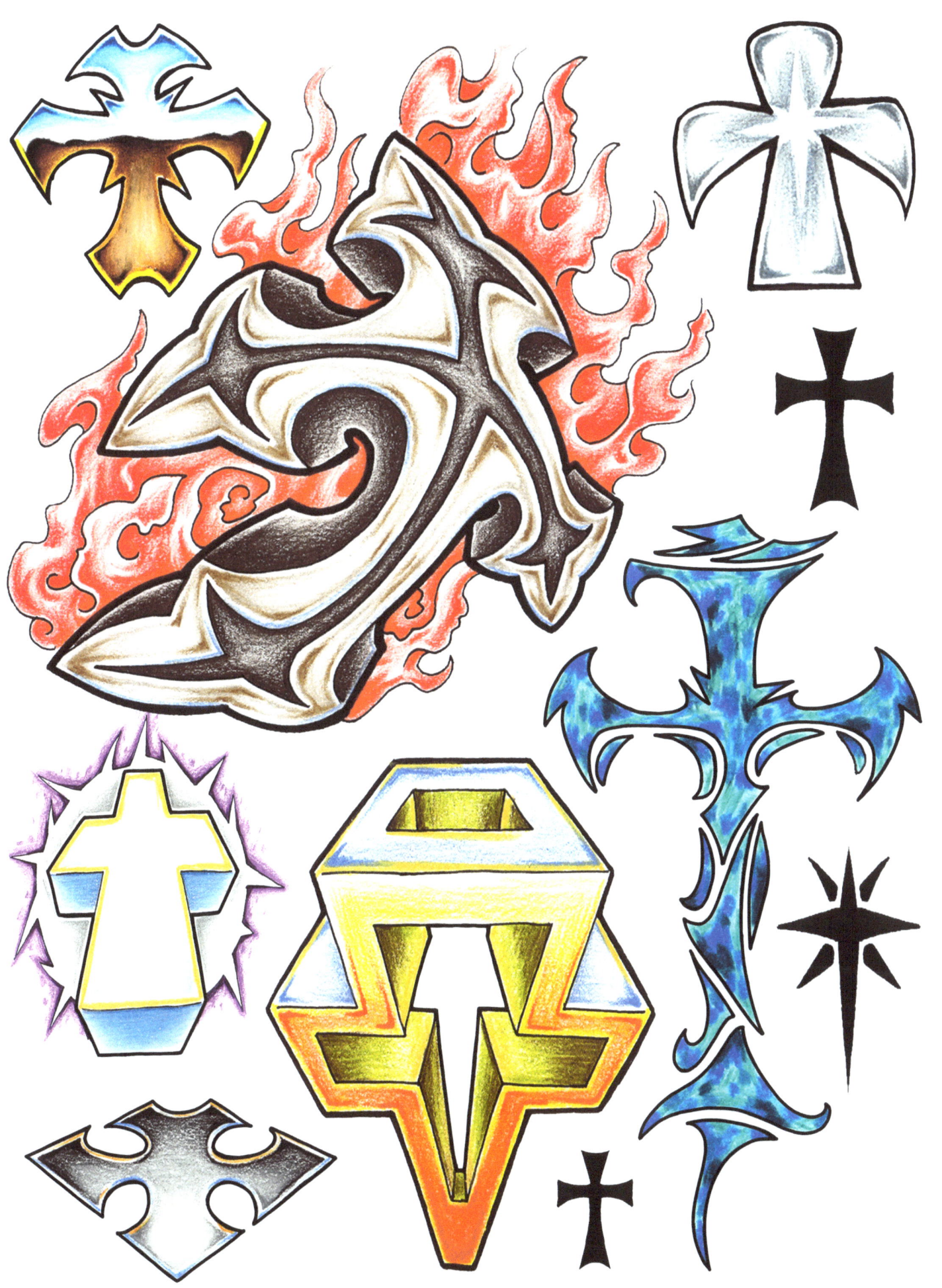

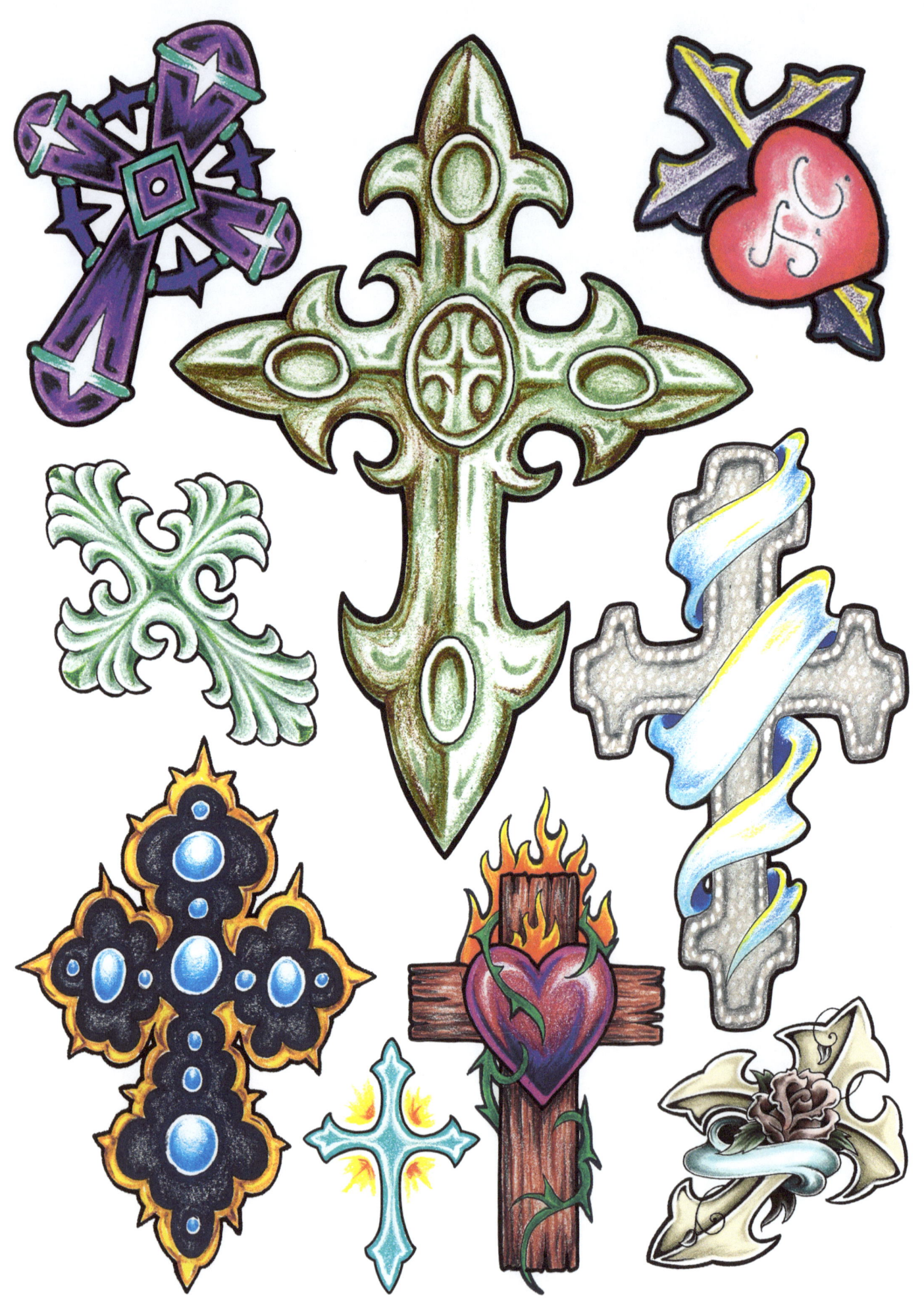

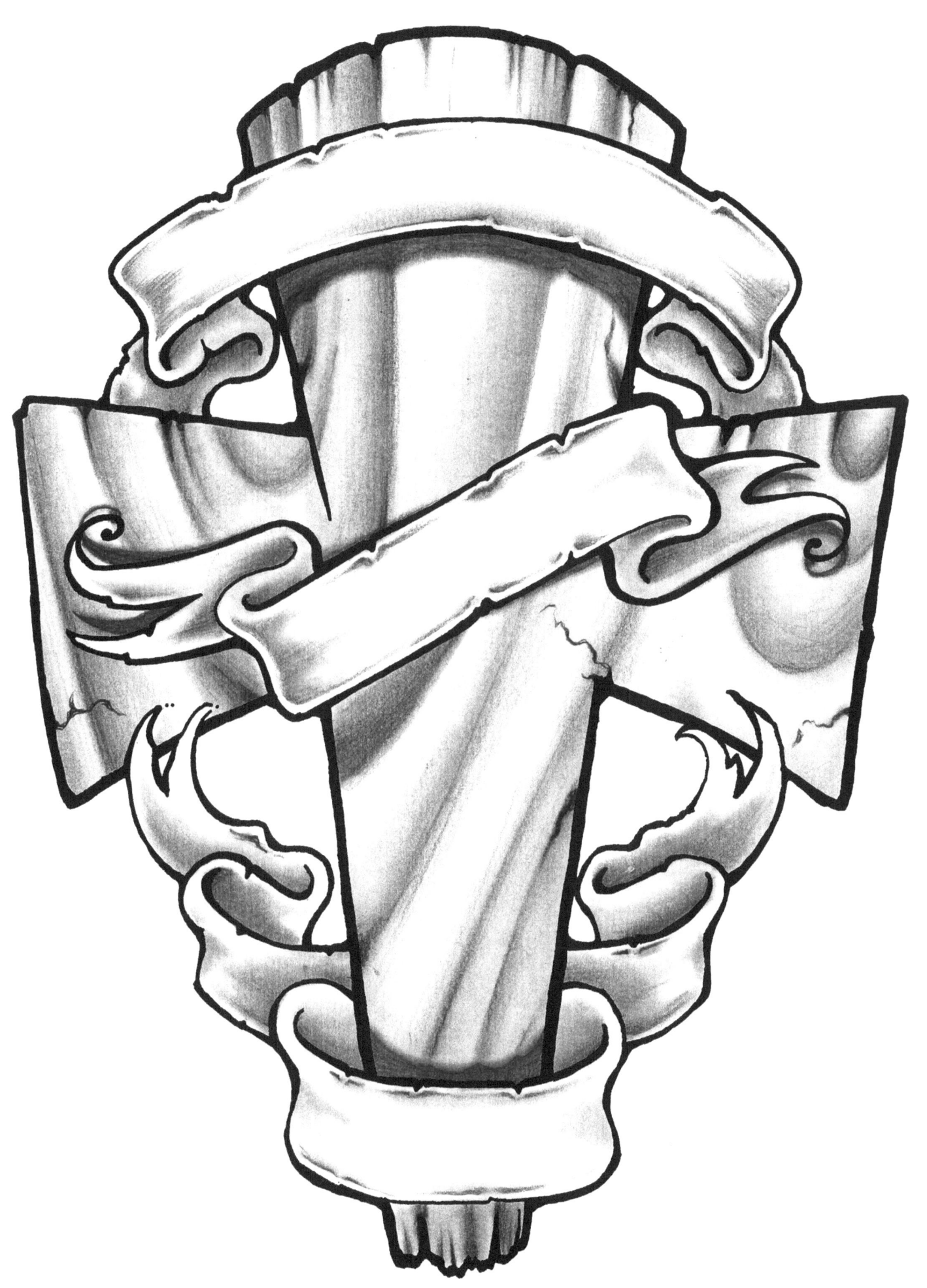

From Japanese style to surreal black and gray, to watercolors and computer art, we have something you will love. Prints ranging in size from 11" x 17" to 40" x 50" will adjust the visual appeal of any room.

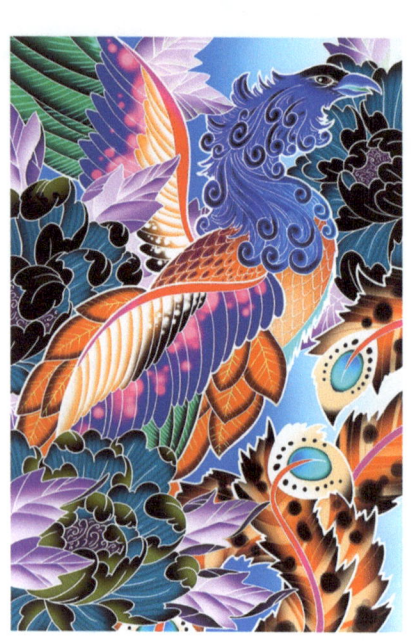
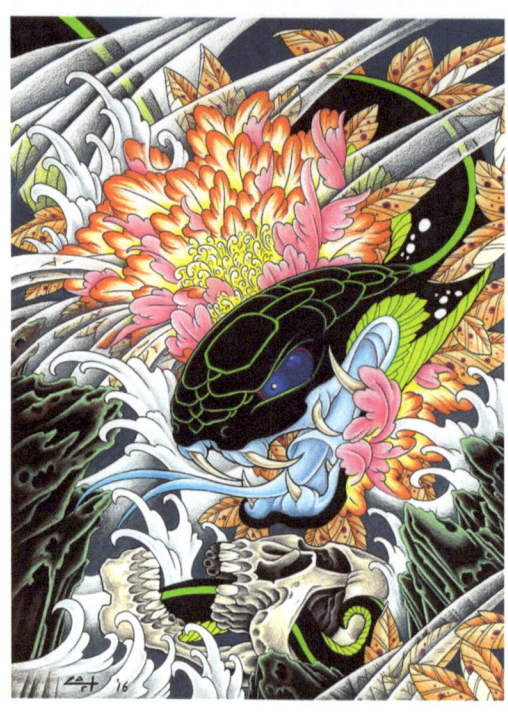
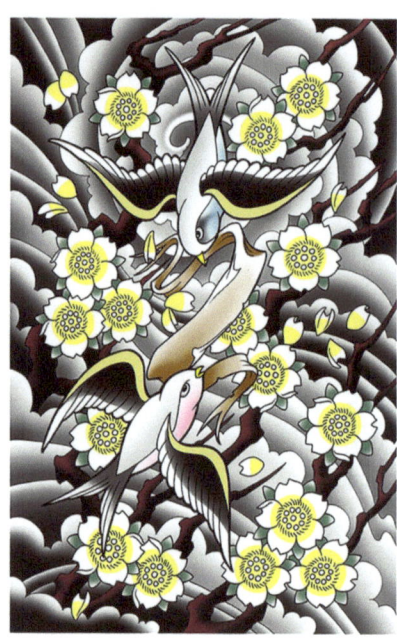
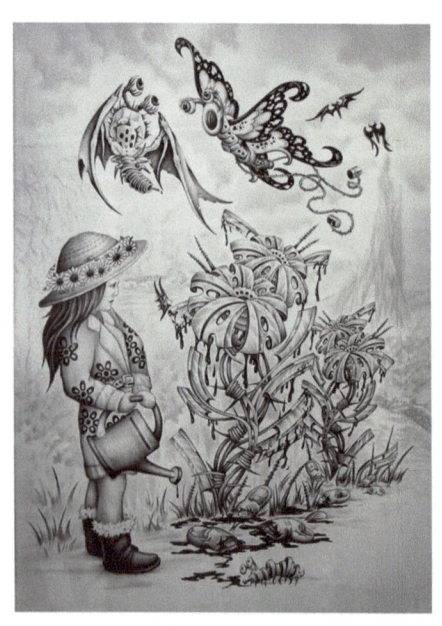
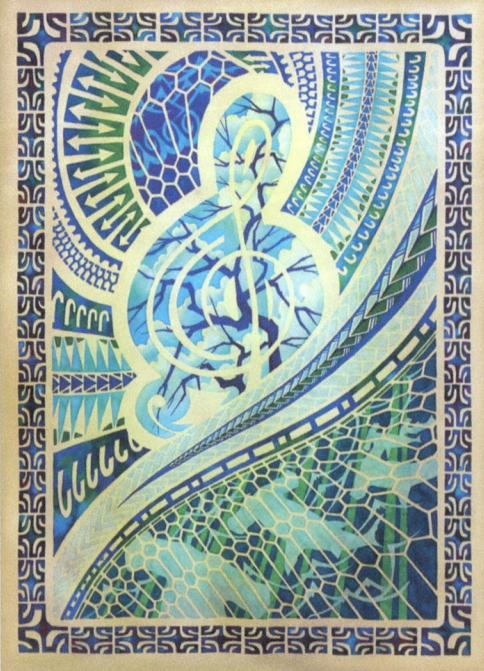
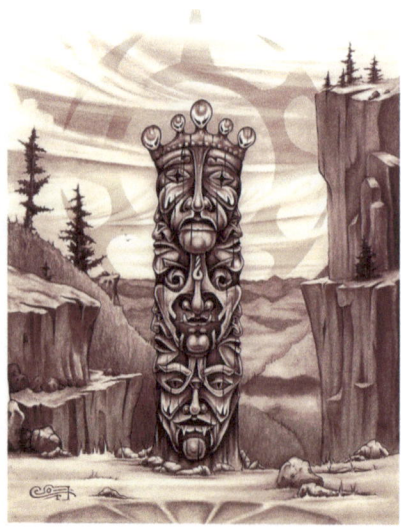

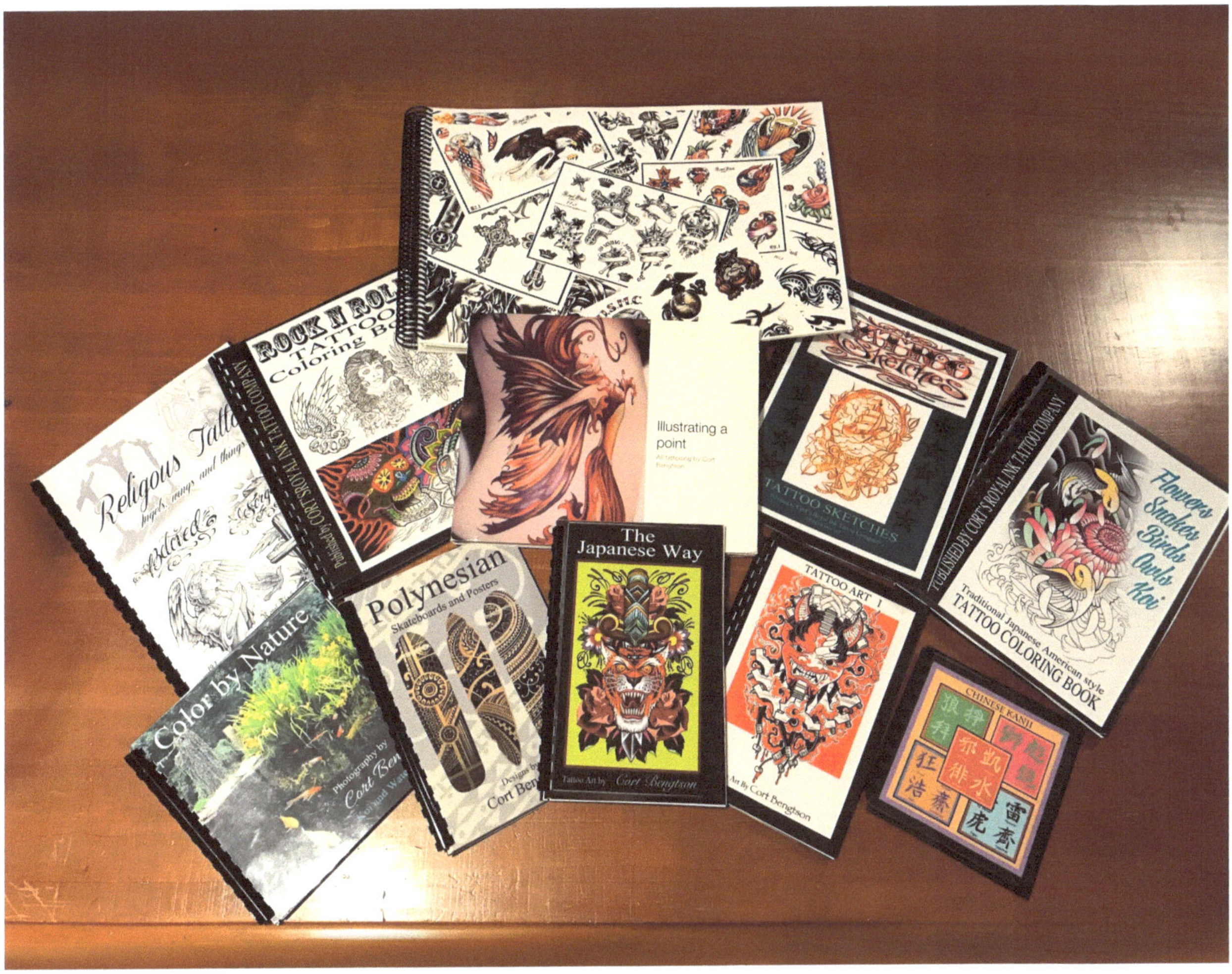

Check out these other great books,
Flash, Prints and original Art from

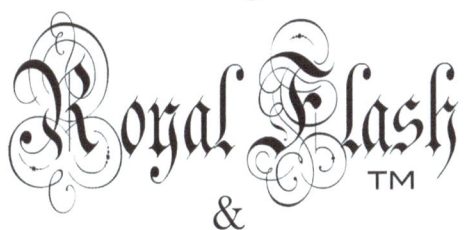

&

Cort's Royal Ink Tattoo Company

@ royalink.631 on ebay

Contact us @ cortsroyalink@aol.com

See whats new @ cortsroyalink on Instagram

COLORKINGTATTOOS.COM

www.ingramcontent.com/pod-product-compliance
Lightning Source LLC
Chambersburg PA
CBHW051203220526
45473CB00003B/887